CRITICAL THEORY OF SOCIETY

CRITICAL THEORY OF SOCIETY

ALBRECHT WELLMER

Translated by John Cumming

A Continuum Book
The Seabury Press · New York

The Seabury Press
815 Second Avenue
New York, N.Y. 10017

First paperback edition 1974

English translation © 1971 by Herder and Herder, Inc.

Original edition: *Kritische Gesellschaftstheorie und Positivismus,*
© 1969 by Suhrkamp Verlag, Frankfurt am Main.

Library of Congress Catalog Card Number: 70-50309
ISBN: 0-8164-9110-0
Printed in the United States of America

CONTENTS

CRITICAL THEORY OF SOCIETY

1. EMPIRICO-ANALYTICAL AND CRITICAL SOCIAL SCIENCE

1.

In the mid-thirties Max Horkheimer wrote a series of articles for the *Zeitschrift für Sozialforschung*[1] in which he set out the principles of the Frankfurt school of sociology as understood by its proponents, who had already been forced out of Germany. At that time capitalist Europe seemed still to be faced with a plain choice between revolution and barbarism; yet the only conceivable instrument of revolution, despite its apparent collapse in the face of German fascism and despite the authoritarian temper and bureaucratic rigidity of the Communist parties under Stalinism, was the international proletariat, whose class solidarity had not yet wholly disappeared under the benefits of a regenerated, state-interventionist capitalism. Understandably, the young Frankfurt sociologists and philosophers, seeing themselves as the intellectual conscience of the Marxist left, still made the criticism of political economy the central component of their theory. In a situation in which the fear and misery of the masses were as palpable as the necessity of pinning one's hopes to a revolutionary outbreak of class conflict, these Marxist theorists could unequivocally view their theoretical work as part of a revolutionary struggle—as its critical self-consciousness.

1. These articles have now been published in collected form in Max Horkheimer, *Kritische Theorie*, 2 vols. (Frankfurt, 1968).

Probably Horkheimer himself offered the most impressive statement of the Frankfurt school's estimate of its own function and importance when, in his article on traditional and "critical" theory,[2] he joined issue with bourgeois science and its objectivist misconception of its own nature. The essay shows clearly that the confrontation between critical, Marxist and traditional "bourgeois" science had hardly moved by then into the vague realm of methodological abstractions; to the extent that the debate was concerned with methodology, critical theory was more inclined to view it as the mere reflection of actual social conflicts. Hence when Horkheimer accuses bourgeois science and philosophy of failing to examine their own socio-practical assumptions and implications, and, therefore, of conforming mutely to the ends of capitalist society, he does not do so in the liberal expectation that it will be possible by reasoned argument critically to analyze and resolve the conception of its own role inherent in bourgeois science—its preoccupation with an objectivist notion of theory. Instead, he posits the impossibility of resolving theoretical differences to the extent that and so long as they are stated exclusively in academic terms and determined solely by academic debate. He realizes that only the political struggle itself and the corresponding process of transformation of the *status quo,* and of the political consciousness of those engaged in the conflict, can produce the instances of verification and falsification, and the possibilities of experience, that will ultimately decide the fate of critical theory.

Horkheimer describes the relation between cognition and interest as follows: "Even if critical theory avoids all arbitrary and fortuitous procedure, the dominant mode of evaluation . . . considers it to be subjective and speculative, partial and unprofitable. Since it runs counter to current and conventional

2. *Zeitschrift für Sozialforschung,* VI, 2, 1937. The page references in subsequent notes are to the text as first published, but I also cite in parentheses the corresponding pages of *Kritische Theorie,* II, where the alterations to the text are negligible.

conceptual models—the guarantors of a partisan world, adhering as they do to a perpetuation of the past and serving the ends of an evanescent order—critical theory appears partisan and unjust." [3] Only the proletariat, which directly experiences as material want the irrationality of the existing society, the "contradiction" between the forces and conditions of production, can discover in critical theory the self-consciousness of its political struggle: but not as if the situation of the proletariat were a "guarantee of true knowledge." [4] With the wisdom gained from participation in a partly crushed and partly bureaucratized socialist movement, Horkheimer insists much more firmly than Marx that the fate of the revolution is decided in the formative process of political struggle: that is, whether it will really be brought to pass "by the conscious will" of the *masses,* and whether the proletariat will attain to a proper consciousness of its situation and the goals before it, depends on the gradually successful even if necessarily fragmentary or interrupted process of anticipation of a rational society available in the organization of the political struggle: "Something of the freedom and spontaneity of the future appears in the organization and community of those engaged in the fight, despite all the disciplinary measures required by the absolute need to prevail. Wherever the unity of discipline and spontaneity has vanished, the movement becomes a concern of its own bureaucracy—a drama already relegated to the repertory of modern history." [5] But the fate of the theory is decided together with the fate of the revolution. Not the judgment of scholars in the same field, but the assent of men who "speak and act for it," is the yardstick by which the historic significance of the theory will be measured.[6]

Horkheimer fully recognized that a changed historical situation (which he thought of as a stage in monopoly capitalism)

3. *Ibid.,* 271 (p. 167).
4. *Ibid.,* 267 (p. 162).
5. *Ibid.,* 271 (p. 166).
6. *Ibid.,* 273 (p. 169).

required a corresponding development of critical theory. Equally, in common with his generation of Marxist intellectuals, he was able to enlist the aid of the "original foundations" of Marxist theory in attacking both bourgeois science and the stultification of Communist orthodoxy. It was still possible then to see the situation as one in which the economic crisis-mechanism of capitalist society *had* to produce the proletariat as deliberate collective poverty and destitution, and consequently as its own grave-digger. The criticism of political economy could therefore claim that by analyzing the illusion of bourgeois ideology it was simultaneously providing the vessel of the revolution with a clear picture of its situation and its necessary aims. On the other hand, it was possible to counter orthodox Communism's dominant determinist or élitist and activist interpretations of the expected change in world history by recourse to Marx himself—to, of course, a "dialectical" Marx insight into whom had been made really keen only by the disappointment of revolutionary hopes. For Horkheimer, the rediscovery of Marx the dialectician means as well the rehabilitation of a significant concept of reason, which, originating in the philosophical tradition, came into its own only with the Marx who, in this respect, was indebted to Hegel. This notion implied the immanent direction of the historical process itself towards men's autonomy in relation to the history they have made; towards the freedom of every individual and the acknowledgement by each man of every other man as a person; and, in short, towards a transcendence of the historic relationship of coercion by a joining of all men in dialogue and common action without constraint.

This concept of reason, which Marx interpreted as a task for political action, was applied in Horkheimer's critique of bourgeois philosophy and science against the instrumental ends-means rationality dominant in capitalist society on account of its antagonistic nature, and against the false conception of the subject-object relation and the connection between theory and practice allied to this particular kind of reasoning. There is

12

here an intimation of the shifting of the political debate on to the level of a discussion of methodology which characterizes recent controversies between critical and analytical theorists. A basic element of Jürgen Habermas's argument is already apparent in the early writings of Horkheimer: he interprets the causally explicative sciences, in accordance with their logical structure, as technically utilizable, and fully acknowledges their liberating significance. Their development is directly related to the prodigious development of the forces of production in capitalist society, which, together with a cumulative increase in control over nature and the destruction of all deep-rooted conditions of life, offers men the objective prerequisites for their social emancipation. In addition, Horkheimer recognizes the objectivistic illusion to which the so-called empirico-analytical sciences have succumbed as the necessary expression of the corresponding scientific *intentio recta*. This appearance of objectivism remains harmless so long as it obscures only for those scientists whose communication is purely within their own field a common interest in reason, the universality of which is the very guarantee of the intersubjectivity of their communication. Since this community of interest expresses an identity of the human species as a whole in contradistinction to an objectified nature, whose conquest through the artifice of social work is a condition of collective survival, the objectivism of the empirico-analytical sciences is seen to be a necessary fiction in cognitive and anthropological terms. Accordingly, there is also the possibility of a strict separation of theory from practice, and of science from the applications of science: "Subject and object are firmly separated, even when it becomes apparent that the objective process will be influenced at a later stage by human action; in science the latter is equally assigned to the category of fact. The objective event transcends theory, and its independence of theory is part of its necessity: the observer as such cannot change this in any way." [7] Under the conditions of

7. *Ibid.*, 280 (p. 177).

modern capitalist production, however, the objectivist illusion becomes dangerous when it is extended to all the areas of the various sciences, and is no longer acknowledged as a fiction. In the social sciences this leads to a misrepresentation of the object under scrutiny and to an accommodating conformism on the part of the scientists. Because they no longer see exactly how, "in every act of perception" (Habermas), they remain imprisoned in and take their bearings from the process of social life, they misrepresent human history as a natural process and willingly act out the role assigned them by the capitalist system as useful and "irresponsible" experts whose knowledge can be smoothly integrated in the system's utility structure.

Critical theory, on the other hand, sees in the economically determined necessity of the course of history to date a gradually effective tendency towards a transformation of blind into meaningful necessity. By using each moment, the being and consciousness of men, their real history and its cultural tradition, reciprocally as a key to decypher the meaning of the other, critical theory understands that the liberating tendency cannot "be known without interest" and cannot be made part of "universal consciousness without actual struggle." [8] "Conscious critical behavior is . . . part of the evolution of society. The structure of the historical process as the necessary product of an economic mechanism includes both the protest which arises from it alone, and which is directed against it, and the idea of the self-determination of the human race: the notion, that is, of a state in which man's deeds will no longer be generated by a mechanism but proceed from his own decisions. Evaluation of the necessity of the process to date therefore includes the struggle to transform that blind into a meaningful necessity. To consider the object of theory apart from theory is to falsify the picture; the result is quietism or conformism. Each of its elements presupposes the existence of criticism of, and struggle

8. *Ibid.,* 275 (p. 172).

14

against, the given situation, in a direction determined by the critical approach itself." [9] Horkheimer's argument shows that critical theory cannot and does not aim to settle on the meta-level of pure methodological debate the methodological controversy imposed on it by the self-restriction of bourgeois science. Because it postulates the primacy of fact over method, the "structure of the historical process" becomes for critical theory the decisive methodological argument against bourgeois social science; unlike empirico-analytical theories, critical theory recognizes the meta-theory of method as one of its constituent parts. This union of theory and meta-theory is only another expression of the unity of theory and practice (*praxis*), which critical theory has made its own. In the controversy about method the actual political struggle is reproduced as a battle of minds: accordingly, critical theory treats the expectation of a resolution of this conflict in the pure medium of the mind as a bourgeois illusion.

2.

Horkheimer's attack on the bourgeois science and philosophy of his time features the specific constellation of theory and practice that critical theory laid claim to in the nineteen thirties. As I see it, this constellation resulted from the relatively unbroken continuity of political economy as the central component of theory. If *this* particular presupposition had not become problematical it would have been possible to reproach the other side only for its lack of understanding with regard to critical theory —an incomprehension conditioned, of course, by interest. For "the Marxist categories of class, exploitation, surplus value, profit, pauperization and break-down are parts of a conceptual whole the meaning of which is to be sought not in the reproduction of contemporary society but in its transformation into a

9. *Ibid.*, 280 f. (pp. 177 f.).

proper society." [10] In the shape of critical theory, this conceptual whole revealed the "secret" of reality as that of a social antagonism, *in such a way* that theoretical criticism had simultaneously and distinctly to be conceived as a part of critical *praxis*: in the last resort, theoretical disputes with bourgeois science could be maintained *in practice* only as a form of the class struggle.

This constellation of practice and theory diagnosed by the critical theorists is clearly to the fore in the essay by Horkheimer that I have drawn on so far. Of course the philosophical opponents to whom Horkheimer refers in this instance are for the most part adherents of neo-Kantianism and the sociology of knowledge. The points I want to raise now are more appropriately illustrated by citing another of Horkheimer's articles, in which he examines logical positivism and anticipates the basic arguments of later critical attacks on the analytical theory of science.[11] Nevertheless, in recent years the debates between critical theory and analytical philosophy or scientific theory have so changed in significance that I should like to approach them from a more systematic point of view.

Halfway through the thirties, logical positivism had already reached the end of its initial, radical phase. This stage was characterized by a general attempt to come to terms with metaphysics and in particular with the German philosophical tradition; and by a simultaneous attempt to elevate the empiricist and sensationalist traditions of European philosophy into a "scientific" philosophy made possible—so it seemed—by the progress of mathematical logic. Like the critical theorists, the logical positivists tried to infer from experience that the debate between schools of philosophy differed from the controversies

10. *Ibid.*, 271 (p. 167).
11. "Der neueste Angriff auf die Metaphysik," in *Zeitschrift für Sozialforschung*, VI, I, 1937 (reprinted in Horkheimer, *Kritische Theorie*, II).

of natural science in being closed to arbitration in the court of academic discussion and in proving itself essentially unfruitful. But the conclusions varied as much as the interpretations of this experience: whereas the critical theorists so interpreted the philosophical theories and controversies as to produce a signification extending beyond the philosophical sphere and into real, antagonistic social processes, the logical positivists refused to allow them any meaning at all. Since they insisted on the essential, intersubjectively binding determinability of meaningful problems, it was only logical that they should obtain their criterion for empirical significance entirely from the only academically effective method of determination—the method of controlled observation common in the natural sciences. But I am expounding an early phase of analytical philosophy from the perspective of a later development: the methodological element of the positivist criterion of meaning became apparent only at a later stage of analytical philosophy. Initially there was a preponderance of logico-epistemological formulations (under the influence of the early Wittgenstein—understood more as a sensationalist), by way of which the positivists were presently to pass into the paradoxes of a self-negating philosophical reflection. The accusation of meaninglessness directed against metaphysics as a whole, and formulated as an empiricist criterion of meaning, showed itself to be no more than a still inadequate metaphysical version of the empiricist principle. This finding had to emerge to the extent that the original versions of the empiricist criterion of meaningfulness were shown to be inadequate in regard to the practical research of the theoretical natural sciences they were supposed to justify. The conventionalist and pragmatic inclination of the later Carnap, which might be dated from *Testability and Meaning,* is evidence of the fact that the recent "experiential given" of the logical positivists was the methodically guaranteed progress of the natural sciences— their intersubjectively acknowledged success. The expression of

17

this progress of the natural sciences in terms of principles that would make the scientific process binding as a paradigm for all scientific procedure is a major concern of later analytical scientific theory, which—after the great European witch-hunt—was developed further mainly in the English-speaking world.

At the latest since the early phase of Popper's work, there has been a clear division of analytical scientific theory into two branches: one concerned with the logical reconstruction of scientific languages, and the other with the logico-methodological reconstruction of the research process itself. Both tendencies interpenetrate and correct one another considerably, and converge at decisive points; all the same, it is sensible to distinguish them, since they feature two persistent and originally mutually independent theoretical approaches: the criticism of meaning found in Wittgenstein's *Tractatus Logico-Philosophicus,* which comprises the idea of a reduction of natural languages to one ideal world-correlative language—itself established in terms of linguistic logic; and the logical approach to experimental science of Popper's *Logic of Scientific Discovery.* But the combined approach of linguistic logic and the analysis of meaningfulness in the *Tractatus* leads not only to the language constructs of Carnap's later work, in which he applies the methodological insights of the young Popper in the area of constructive semantics, but to the linguistic philosophy of Wittgenstein's later work, which served as an introduction to the linguistic phase of analytical philosophy.

This very summary and incomplete genealogy of analytical philosophy, from which I have, for instance, excluded the significant influence of Russell and Moore, is intended only to emphasize the systematic value assigned to some fundamental positions of analytical scientific theory that are significant in regard to the controversy about methodology in the social sciences. What is common to these positions can be established from the common scientistic premiss that they explicate. Popper's methodological position, which he developed initially in *The*

Logic of Scientific Discovery,[12] is already dependent on a rejection of the logical positivists' approach through the analysis of meaning: he is concerned not with the distinction between meaningful propositions and meaningless pseudo-propositions, but with the separation of the scientific from the unscientific interpretation of theories: that is, methodologically to distinguish scientific research that qualifies as intersubjectively acknowledged progress, from pseudo-scientific speculation and indoctrination. Popper makes falsifiability the criterion of the scientific status of empirical propositional systems—the criterion of elimination. It is significant that he developed this criterion in direct opposition to Marxism and psychoanalysis; unlike the positivistic criterion of meaningfulness, which retains a genuine, philosophically epistemological, basic approach in the form of the negation of all philosophy, Popper's criterion features the tendency proper to the positivistic theory of science: that is, the intention to make scientific empiricism the unique, consciously applied law of scientific research. Popper's methodology is an explication of this scientific empiricism: scientific theories are systems of universal, empirically falsifiable laws; scientific method is the method of discovery, of empirical testing, and of the further development of empirical theories through falsifications. The aim of scientific theories is the revelation of those structures of reality the knowledge of which will make it possible to explain singular and uncomprehended phenomena: the "explanation" of a phenomenon consists in deduction from specific initial conditions with the aid of a universal law. Causal *explanation,* however, is a subsequent *prognosis;* the peculiar value of scientific theories consists in the possibility of deducing from them general conditioned prognoses, which can be checked against reality. In other words, explanation and prognosis have the same logical structure: a theoretical explanation is checked by testing the prognoses deduced from the theory in question.

12. Karl R. Popper, *Logik der Forschung* (Vienna, 1934); English translation: *The Logic of Scientific Discovery* (London, 1959).

But the main consequence of the unity of structure of explanation and prognosis is that, by virtue of their logical structure, scientific theories are technically utilizable theories: the knowledge of functional relations between variables, or between "causes" and "effects," extends the operational field of possible rational-useful procedure. In a later work, *The Poverty of Historicism*,[13] Popper developed this connection between the logical structure of scientific theories and their technical applicability, which also implies a specific relationship between theory and practice, and between scientific discovery and its practical application. In this book, and in the theses regarding the philosophies of history and sociology in *The Open Society*, Popper gives the positivistic answer to critical theory, by offering a socio-ethical basis for his restriction of the concept of science. In doing so he fundamentally rejects the same deterministic and élitist-activist tendencies of Marxist revolutionary theory that the critical theorists had rejected—though in the opposite direction. To the vices of quietism and revolutionary activism characteristic of "holistic" historicism, he opposes the virtues of an active, self-critical tolerance and restriction to "piecemeal social engineering." Since he already analyzes Marxist theory according to a scientistic pre-valuation, he is able effortlessly to dismiss as unscientific speculation, or mere value judgments, anything in Marxist theory that does not satisfy his methodological standards. In fact, the concept of science advanced by Popper implies a strict separation of factual and value judgments together with a parallelism of theory and practice. If one also follows Popper in deducing from this concept of science a universal yardstick for possible objectivity and rationality, the only status left for the eliminated value judgments is that of subjective, irrational decisions. Accordingly, the determination of practical aims—that is, their applications—would have to be rigorously

13. London, 1957.

20

separated from science itself, and treated in the sphere of politics.

But Popper is obliged to pretend that this extraneous treatment is still possible in the form of coercion-free assent. As a liberal heir of the Enlightenment, he can justify the heteronomy of scientific discovery in relation to the social utility of knowledge only by pretending that society consists of autonomous subjects. In this way, however, Popper ultimately devises a social theory with precisely the "unscientific" reference to practice that critical theory laid claim to. Nevertheless, with its conversion of actual antagonisms into a pluralism of irrational value judgments, the liberal justification of scientism accords not with critical but with conservative theory. It supplies the social engineers of the industrial system with the legitimation of measures in accordance with the dominant value system, which is withdrawn from any effective public discussion: this means—in accordance with the stabilization of the existing social power structure.

Popper's conservatism is the product of his hypostatization of the decision process of the modern empirico-analytical sciences: that is, of the repeatable experiment or the observation rendered intersubjectively testable through operationalization. Still, he is distinguished from most other representatives of analytical scientific theory in that, from the start, unburdened by the presuppositions of the analysis of meaning, he has taken into account the dimension of practical rationality which encroaches upon scientistic rationality—a dimension in which the methodological discussion has also been located. Considering the divergence of theoretical approaches, it is not fortuitous that Popper's theory of science is set in a historical and social philosophy whose reflected union of theoretical and practical-political aims has remained quite alien to the branch of analytical scientific theory drawing its strength from the analysis of meaning.

The comparatively liberal theses of Carnap's later work are also essentially indebted to the suasions of meaning analysis.

21

Carnap's position, as outlined for instance in his article "The Methodological Character of Theoretical Concepts," [14] is relevant to the present discussion for two reasons. One is that Carnap now derives the principle of his constructive criticism of meaning from the methodological criteron of the "prognostic relevance" of concepts, and thus approximates to Popper's position; the other is that Carnap's linguistic-logical approach reveals certain implications of scientific empiricism more clearly than Popper's methodological approach. These implications have found a degree of recognition in the various versions of the thesis of physicalism never generally accorded them to date within the analytical theory of science.

At the latest since *Testability and Meaning,* the equivocation of the charge of meaninglessness laid against metaphysics by the early logical positivists has become quite obvious; it is an equivocation grounded in the pragmatic components of the meaning of "meaning" (*Sinn*). Carnap's pragmatic or conventionalist version consists only in his interpretation of the meaninglessness of metaphysics as its uselessness, and of meaningful as useful language. Hence the quest for an adequate empiricist criterion of meaning produces the quest for expedient principles for the construction of a scientific universal language. For the Carnap of *Testability and Meaning,* the logical reconstructibility of scientific language on the basis of an intersubjectively applied language of physical observation is the decisive criterion of its "usefulness." Later on Carnap was forced to recognize that a reconstruction of this kind was impossible for the language of theoretical physics, and thereby happened upon an important "use" of the language of science—its prognostic potential.

To help illustrate my point, I should like to outline at least the basic elements of Carnap's later construction. Carnap distinguishes an observational language L_o from a theoretical lan-

14. In *Minnesota Studies in the Philosophy of Science I,* ed. H. Feigl and M. Scriven (Minneapolis, 1956).

guage L_T. L_o is posited as an intersubjectively applied language of physical observation. The theoretical language L_T roughly comprises that part of mathematics relevant to empirical science, as well as the descriptive terms that cannot be introduced with the aid of observational predicates. Accordingly, a *theory* consists of a finite series of postulates formulated in the theoretical language L_T, and can be apprehended as a logical conjunction of these postulates. Every theory is primarily an uninterpreted system; the theoretical terms obtain a merely indirect and incomplete empirical interpretation inasmuch as some of them are united by means of "rules of correspondence" with observational predicates, and the remaining terms are united with the first set by means of theoretical postulates. The rules of correspondence make possible the deduction of observational propositions from theoretical propositions, or of theoretical propositions from observational propositions.

The important conclusion for the formulation of an empiricist criterion of meaning is that such a criterion for theoretical terms can still be formulated only in regard to a theory T; in other words, the significance of theoretical terms depends on the configuration of these terms in a system of postulates. To avoid unnecessary technical detail, I shall repeat Carnap's criterion in a simplified version, as represented by Stegmüller [15]: "A theoretical concept of T, which is neither through definitions nor rules of correspondence wholly or partly reducible to observation, must possess, in order to be characterized as empirically admissible, a *predictive relevance* or a *prognostic relevance*. Roughly, this means that there must at least be an assertion of T, containing this concept, with the aid of which predictions of future observable events can be inferred."

The guiding principle of Carnap's construction implies that scientific theories must have an intersubjectively testable prognostic content. For Carnap, this intersubjectivity, of theoretical

15. W. Stegmüller, *Hauptströmungen der Gegenwartsphilosophie* (Stuttgart, 1960), p. 456.

language as well, is guaranteed by means of an actually applied, intersubjectively unambiguous language of physical observation. For Carnap, the observational language is "theory-free" in the sense that the meaning of its elementary descriptive constants is free from theoretical assumptions; the elementary terms are not further analyzable within the language of science as delimited by the empiricist criterion, and their signification is constant. Of course, Carnap acknowledges the independence from theory of observational language as fictitious, but maintains that this fiction is pragmatically meaningful: it indicates the "fortunate empirical fact" that there is such a thing as a functioning, extensional, observational language, whose statements are understood in the same sense by all members of a language community, and in which, therefore, comprehension is always technically possible. The existence of this language guarantees the intersubjectivity of the scientific language constructed on its basis.

In *The Logic of Scientific Discovery,* Popper also related the intersubjectivity of the empirical content of theories to an observational language functioning in practice, and even disclosed the secret of its acquisition; which is synonymous with the acquisition of certain techniques of measurement and experimentation. It is the ordinary language of technical control of the objectified processes of the world of natural and social life. Only Carnap's attempt to analyze the logical relations between observational language and theoretical language reveals the physicalist implications or, rather, presuppositions of scientific empiricism, which Popper, for instance, refuses to acknowledge. This is evident in Carnap's interpretation of the language of "mental events." *Testability and Meaning* contains a chapter on "psychological" concepts in which Carnap advocates so-called "introspection" rather than radical behaviorism as a permissible mode of observation, even though it is restricted on account of its "subjective nature." Accordingly, predicates which, for example, describe psychic conditions can be classed as scientific language. But there was a consensus of opinion, within

24

analytical scientific theory as well, that propositions concerning psychic conditions or events could not be translated into propositions about (actual or possible) external behavior. If Carnap accepts introspection as a variety of observation, he errs: as predicates of the language of science, psychological concepts are theoretical terms the application of which can be indirectly and incompletely controlled by means of behaviorist tests; only in introspection is it possible—in a private sense—to approximate them to observational terms. The elementary constants of observational language, in accordance with our foregoing interpretation, in any meaningful sense can only be predicates of physical object-language. But this requires an interpretation of intentional languages which has serious consequences: logically, they are locatable in a linguistic world construct that is raised exclusively on the basis of the functions of the explanation and prognosis of physical events.[16] Accordingly, Carnap keeps to a modified form of the physicalism thesis, which would now assert that all scientific theories, inclusive of psychological theories, are ultimately reducible to microphysical theories.

Unlike that out-of-date liberal Popper, Carnap is an uncompromising representative of the technocratic consciousness of his own times. One might even say that he has taken the linguistic-critical approach of the young Wittgenstein to just as radical a conclusion as Wittgenstein himself. If Wittgenstein in his later work deciphers the meaning of language in its practical functioning, Carnap rejects as meaningless any language which does not function faultlessly; if Wittgenstein asserts the unity of language and forms of life, Carnap divines the difference remaining between them—and applies himself to remove it. He remedies the practical impotence of the still unreified consciousness by contributing constructively to the desiccation of the still un-technified areas of language; and he gives a helping hand to

16. Cf. H.-J. Giegel, *Die Logik der seelischen Ereignisse* (Frankfurt, 1969), pp. 60 f.

the individual (whose infirmity now has a longish history) by integrating him in a uniform intersubjectivity in which no "I" can persist.[17]

Admittedly, this is an ironic approximation of Carnap to the later Wittgenstein. In fact, Carnap and Wittgenstein drew radically different conclusions from the failure of all attempts to justify in terms of language-criticism the world-correlative universal language of the natural sciences as the only meaningful language. Whereas Carnap tries constructively to apply the metaphysical fiction of the world-correlative common language, and thus to abrogate the multiplicity of everyday languages, the late Wittgenstein is deeply concerned with this very difference: in it he discovers the functional richness of actual languages together with the multiplicity of linguistic modes which they contain and which are irreducible to the unique mode of objectifying description: "There are . . . countless different kinds of use of what we call 'symbols,' 'words,' 'sentences.' And this multiplicity is not something fixed, given once for all; but new types of language, new language-games, as we may say, come into existence, and others become obsolete and get forgotten."[18] But if the reductive reference of natural language to a world-correlative ideal language is shown to be impossible, then the conditions for language analysis change altogether. In other words, it is now apparent that the explication of ordinary languages is possible only in the dimension of these languages themselves. This circle, in which any understanding and any explication of language is comprised, indicates however that the acquisition of language is bound up with the acquisition of a form of existence: language is part of an activity, or form, of life. The grammatical rules of language constitute a form of

17. Cf. J. Habermas, *Zur Logik der Sozialwissenschaften* (Tübingen, 1967), pp. 156 f.

18. *Philosophical Investigations,* trans. G. E. M. Anscombe, 3rd ed. (London, 1967), 23 (p. 11).

social reality; in other words, the grammatical rules are necessarily more than *mere* grammatical rules; inasmuch as they govern a *praxis,* they are also rules of training in a social form of life.[19]

Hence Wittgenstein recognizes the different "language-games" as different forms of existence. By revealing the illusion conjured up by the nominalist explanation of language, and by establishing the meaning of words and sentences in the rules of their actual usage, he is able to decypher the grammars of language-games not only as forms of apprehension of the world, but as forms of social reality. But this results in serious objections to the basic intentions of scientific empiricism. Firstly, the language-game of natural science becomes one language-game among others, which also means: one form of life among others. Secondly, social science is also directly rescued from the methodological embrace of the unique universal science, and located immediately next to philosophy as the "administratrix of grammar"; for: "the logical analysis of ordinary language encounters . . . , in the grammar of forms of life, the field of study of the social sciences themselves." [20] In accordance with its innermost structure, this field of investigation resists the objectifying procedure of a science whose epistemological aim is the confirmation of mere "regularities," or uniformities; it can be comprehended only by the uncovering of those grammatical rules which constitute a particular form of life as it is lived. But this is possible only from "within": that is, only by means of the sociologist's communication with and participation in the world of social life that he is investigating. As language-analysis, quasi-transcendentally, becomes direct empirical analysis, so sociology as interpretative sociology becomes specific language-analysis.

Peter Winch has drawn these radical methodological conclu-

19. Cf. Habermas, *op. cit.,* pp. 124 ff.
20. *Ibid.,* p. 133.

sions from the later linguistic philosophy of Wittgenstein.[21] Winch's position is significant because it represents an extreme counter-position to behaviorism and to empirico-analytical social research as a whole, and yet is descended from the self-reflection of analytical philosophy itself. Winch compares the attitude of the social scientist to the phenomenon which he investigates with that of the natural scientist, who has a common mode of communication with his fellow-scientists participating in the process of research as the same *general* kind of learned activity: it is the attitude of the participant in a game who understands the particular mode of the game. According to Winch, this attitude is necessarily imposed on the social scientist by the structure of the object of his investigation, because the facts of social reality have a meaning grounded in themselves—in their internal relations: they are constituted as fragments of an activity or form of life which is itself governed by rules.

But the investigator can attain to this "particular meaning" of social facts only by means of the self-understanding of the active subjects of the particular social form of life, inasmuch as he participates in their mode of communication; and this implies a change in the nature of the verification and falsification of hypotheses: the effectiveness of a meaning cannot be verified by experiments but, ultimately, only by successful interaction. Therefore the structure of the field of investigation itself demonstrates the radical inappropriateness of a social science that relies on behavioristic procedure. The behavioristic alienation of social reality abrogates its social character: "Hence actions are formed in the contexts of linguistically mediated interactions in such a way that an intersubjectively valid meaning is 'embodied' in the observable modes of behavior. Consequently, a sociology of interpretative understanding uses an essentially language-critical approach, and apprehends the norms which govern behavior by a study of the rules of ordinary, or natural, com-

21. Peter Winch, *The Idea of a Social Science and Its Relation to Philosophy* (London, 1958).

munication [which that behavior exemplifies]. This again shows the way in which the construction of theories depends on the self-understanding of the subjects—the persons whose behavior is in question." [22]

Of course, Winch's outline of a language-interpretative sociology on the basis of the philosophy of the later Wittgenstein leads to a theoretical difficulty to which Habermas has drawn attention. Wittgenstein conceives language-games as monadic unities; he has discarded the idea of the unique language together with that of the ideal common language transcendentally prior to all natural languages. He transfers the inclusiveness of the unique language divided into a multiplicity of language-games to the individual language-games themselves. In so doing, he does not, admittedly, wholly deny the reciprocal practical translatability of different languages, but he does, in a special way, negate the reflexivity of natural languages and the possibility of self-transcendence guaranteed by this reflexivity: in other words, the intentional tendency to universal translatability contained in each of them. Wittgenstein rediscovered the "perfect order" of the ideal language in the perfect order of ordinary languages (of admittedly complex structure). The unbroken intersubjectivity of these languages is that of the logical ideal language itself. But since ordinary languages would be reduced by that dimension in which they transcend themselves in only an intermittently intersubjective form, a reflexive language analysis could only represent as a demonstrable meaning what was already fully covered by a rule-governed activity or form of life. But then the meaning of the analysis could still be determined only in a negative-practical manner in contrast to the practical functioning of everyday language—as an "ordering" of language in order to restore a pathologically disturbed form of communication. The propositions of the *Philosophical Investigations* are inauthentic propositions, possessing not a descriptive but merely a therapeutic significance. This revocation of his own philosophical discourse

22. Habermas, *op. cit.*, p. 135.

is an indication of the continuity in Wittgenstein's work between the *Tractatus* and the *Philosophical Investigations*. For Wittgenstein, philosophy is radically practical; it leaves everything as it is.

But this shows that it is impossible to have a language-interpretative sociology without going beyond the bounds imposed by Wittgenstein's conception. Sociology requires a theoretical and not merely linguistic-therapeutic approach. Hence it needs a meta-language to mediate the analyzed language-games—with the language of the social investigator as well as with one another. And so it represents a new language-game in itself, the possibility of which alone implies the intention to enquire behind the meaning apparent in the immanent logic of each language—implies the tendency to become theory. Winch takes this possibility of a language-interpretative sociology into account, but without examining its prerequisites: the breaching of the monadic compactness of language-games in the historical dimension of language as a nexus of tradition; the applicative function of an interpretative social theory in regard to the situation and the self-understanding of the investigator, and the practical cognitive interest of an interpretative sociology apparent in this. Instead, Winch repeats the objectivism of analytical scientific theory on the level of its socio-linguistic self-reflection. As Habermas has demonstrated, Winch's conception of an interpretative sociology is a linguistic version of historicism. But this contradiction of Wittgenstein's conception reveals the dilemma inherent in it: from the viewpoint of sociological theory, Wittgenstein's reflections prevented not only the possibility of a behavioristic alienation of social reality, but the interpretative application of the theory. These difficulties of a language-interpretative sociology according to Winch's model ultimately reveal the boundary of Wittgenstein's philosophy of language itself: it is the boundary beyond which hermeneutics lies and which Wittgenstein did not cross.

30

3.

In spite of the theoretical dilemmas in which it becomes enmeshed, the approach of language-analytical interpretative sociology does call in question the dominant presupposition of the methodical absolutism of analytical scientific theory. This presupposition consists in asserting that no argument can be obtained *a priori* from the structure of the phenomena of social investigation to be directed against the universal profitability of the empirico-analytical method, since this method is, without exception, the only proficient means of uncovering the structures of reality. Of course, Wittgenstein's and Winch's deliberations have not been able seriously to affect the self-consciousness of empirico-analytical social science, which is based not on philosophical reflections but on the results of practical research, which by the very fact of their existing at all would seem to reduce Winch's radical methodological standpoint to nil. In fact, the mere *possibility* of an empirico-analytical social science is at least just as forceful an argument against Winch's position as the very inconsistency of that position itself. If, therefore, immanent criticism is to go beyond Winch (and hence at the same time beyond analytical theory), two directions are indicated: (1) a methodological restriction of Winch's conception; and (2) its hermeneutical extension. Habermas has criticized language-interpretative sociology along these lines. By relating both critical tendencies, he tries to transcend both an empirico-analytical and a language-interpretative sociology, and to project both into the concept of a critical social theory.

I cannot reproduce Habermas's critique in detail here, but I should like to summarize the results that seem most important in the context of the present debate, even though at times this will necessitate a somewhat stark paraphrase of his highly nuanced argument.

If one disregards the actual attachment of hermeneutical

philosophy to the history of thought (*Geistesgeschichte*), it is possible to follow Habermas and Apel in recognizing in hermeneutical consciousness what is (in contrast to Wittgenstein's linguistic philosophy) a possible new stage of positivistic self-reflection, attained upon perceiving the "imprecision" (also confirmed by Wittgenstein) of ordinary language games as the decisive argument against the notion of their monadic autonomy. Unlike formalized languages, ordinary, or natural, languages would then experience the dimension of the application of grammatical rules as the dimension of their development too. But in this way language simultaneously attains to a new dimension: that of history. Thus Habermas assigns a systematic location to Gadamer's theories (which he refers to extensively): "For Gadamer, language achieves a third dimension: grammar controls an application of rules which, for its own part, extends systems of rules historically. The unity of language lost in the plurality of language-games is dialectically restored in the context of tradition. Language *is* only as language is handed down. For tradition reflects on a larger scale the socialization of individuals in their language, a socialization which extends throughout their lifetime." [23]

This historical dimension of language is, however, that of the area of study of social science, and therefore the dimension of social science itself. I shall now indicate the implications of this: (1) for the possible significance of an interpretative sociology; and (2) for an empirico-analytical practical sociology.

1. One of the most important contributions of hermeneutical thought is the destruction of the objectivistic pretensions of the historico-hermeneutical sciences, among which a language-interpretative sociology might be counted. By seeing the scientist and the object of his research as linked by a context of tradition, hermeneutical thought discovers in the process of mediation (that is: the interpretative explication of historically

23. Habermas, *op. cit.*, p. 155.

evolving forms of life), the practical life-interests which, as such, cannot be discarded and are operative in the scientist's initial insight. His interpretations and explanations exist as such in the perspective of future behavior, and are offered from the boundary of his historical situation. Even though his preliminary attitude may change in the process of critical appreciation of traditions, or of the decoding of initially alien significant links, he can neither entirely escape from the total context of tradition (upon which even the most reflective form of "appreciation" must ultimately be brought to bear), nor wholly free himself from the nexus by which this tradition relates to his own future. Consequently, his indications remain suggestions, which have to be proven not only in regard to the material already available, but in the future historical practice of human beings from which the thread of tradition continues and will continue to be formed.

As it destroys the illusive appearance of objectivity, hermeneutic thought also reveals the factual *limits* of a purely subjective interpretative sociology. The latter "explains social behavior in terms of motives which are identical with the subject's own assessments of situation, and therefore with the linguistically articulated meaning, or verbal statement, by which he orientates himself." [24] But even linguistic analysis recognizes that "explanation" in terms of motives is not causal explanation, but a form of description: motive and action are not related as cause and effect. Hermeneutical thought also recognizes that conceivable meaning is not necessarily subjectively intended meaning; and that the real meaning of actions is not necessarily identical with their subjectively intended meaning. Therefore, an interpretative sociology cannot be restricted to the description of subjectively intended contexts of meaning. In contrast to purely language-analytical interpretative sociology, hermeneutical theory justifies attempts at a functionalist, ideology-critical or psychoanalytical description of objectively meaningful social relations.

24. Habermas, *op. cit.*, p. 182.

To summarize: In contrast to the positivistic attempt to reduce intentional behavior to observable behavior, that is, to describe social facts as natural facts and, in *this* way, to integrate the social sciences in the "unified science" of empirical analysis, the theory of linguistic analysis established the relative autonomy of intentional action in regard to the area of non-intentional natural processes; the originality of the contribution made by linguistic analysis consists in the demonstration of the connection between the concept of "rule following" and that of intentionality. The contribution of hermeneutical thought, on the other hand, is to be found in its disclosure of the objectivistic illusion that necessarily restricts a language-analytical interpretative sociology of the type represented by Winch: in other words, in "its pursuit, on the basis of operational history, of a communicative access to the field of study of the social sciences." [25] By perceiving that the monadic autonomy of language-games is a fiction, hermeneutical thought discovers too that "meaning can be experienced even when it is not fulfilled as intended"; [26] in other words: it reveals the limitations of a purely subjective meaning-analysis sociology.

2. On the other hand, hermeneutical theory implies a criticism of the self-conception of the empirico-analytical social sciences which, in contrast to Winch's linguistic-analytical critique, allows these sciences the partial justification to which they can be shown to be entitled. Since hermeneutical theory sees the falsity of the premiss that the meaningful structure of the objective field of the social sciences is at the same time composed solely of subjectively intended (because intersubjectively valid) meaning, it recognizes the legitimacy of the attempt to reveal something of this structure by recording purely empirical regularities according to the pattern of the natural sciences.

25. H.-G. Gadamer, "Rhetorik, Hermeneutik und Ideologiekritik," in *Kleine Schriften* I (Tübingen, 1967), p. 120.
26. *Ibid.*, p. 122.

More important, however, is the criticism of the self-conception of the empirico-analytical social sciences themselves. Here I can refer only to a few important points in Habermas's detailed critique.

Apart from strict behaviorists, social scientists would in general no longer dispute the fact that access to the measured or observed *data* of their field of study is obtained through the medium of communication. But, they opine, the role of interpretation finishes with its provision of a means of access to the data, and perhaps also of a heuristic value for the discovery of explanations; in addition, they would claim for their science the methodological status of a natural science, and therefore of a science entitled, with the aid of universal laws, to explain and predict unusual phenomena. On the basis of this self-conception, they explain two particular difficulties confronting empirico-analytical social science, as mere preliminary or technical problems arising from the relatively undeveloped state of this science. One difficulty is that to date no one has discovered any really universal social laws, and that, where they have been thought to have been uncovered, they have lost all specifically social contents and consequently all specifically social explanatory value. To a certain extent, the situation in the social sciences would appear to be the converse of that obtaining in physical science: the more universal the laws, the more devoid of content they become, or rather: the less explanatory value they have. The second difficulty is the result of the attempt to measure social facts: there is no satisfactory and universally valid operationalization of theoretical principles in the social sciences.

Both difficulties are actually problems of principle, and result from the basic hermeneutical situation of the researcher and the meaningful structure of his field of study. Cicourel has demonstrated the problem of measurement.[27] The basic consideration is simply that since the theoretical framework of reference must

27. A. V. Cicourel, *Method and Measurement in Sociology* (Glencoe, 1964).

CRITICAL THEORY OF SOCIETY

relate to the pre-interpretation arising from the process of communication in a social world, there must always be a pre-existing relationship between the basic theoretical predicates and the observable data, which, because it does not derive from arbitrary operational procedures, cannot be recovered by such procedures. Consequently, operationalizations are *ad hoc:* they can be more or less appropriate, but in principle they are always subject to revision. However, this also means that the researcher *cannot* relegate the communicative relationship with his observational field to a preliminary stage in his own particular scientific work. Automatically, it continually obtrudes itself upon him so long as he lays claim to any social relevance for his theories. The implications of this finding can best be seen in an extreme counter-model. The researcher who would rely once and for all on the operational procedures chosen on a single occasion, would run the danger of being able at best, with the aid of his theories, to explain and predict certain observable events that could no longer be translated back into events of a specific social world. Consequently, even from the most limited standpoint (that of social engineering), his theories would be practically worthless, and "speechless" in the literal sense. This particular difficulty does not arise in the natural sciences, where the intersubjectively binding content of theoretical statements occurs on the level of—universally applicable—measurement operations themselves, and does not have to be continually verified anew in a process of communication with an intrinsically significant object.

The other problem has an analogous cause: So much of the specific content of a certain historical period enters into the basic theoretical assumptions and the framework of reference used for categorization, that its hypotheses cannot be transferred without violence to more distant socio-historical situations. The measurement problem recurs on a world-historical scale: either the basic theoretical predicates obtaining in supposedly universal laws are, with the aid of a general reference, introduced into world-historical measurement operations: in which case these assumptions lose both their specific historic content (which cannot be saved by means of general "rules of correspondence," because the correspondence between both predetermined methods of description—the one operationally general and the other historically concrete—is precisely what *is* problematical), *and* their socio-historical explanatory power; or, the generality of the hypothesis is the result of an abstract generalization: in which case they degenerate to become abstract basic assumptions of a theoretical frame of reference with any empirical explanatory value.

However, in both these dilemmas it is evident that empirico-analytical social science is laboring under a misapprehension if it sees itself as a special branch of a unified science defined according to the pattern of physical science. For the consequences of these difficulties are not ultimately methodological. Obviously, empirical social science cannot employ a universally meaningful research strategy if it aims to trace known regularities with a restricted historical range back to increasingly general and ultimately historically neutral laws. In physical science, as Popper has shown, this research strategy implies a continual increase in the empirical content of its theories; in social science, however, as a rule the exact contrary is the case. Hence it is clear that the technical cognitive interest which is constitutive for the natural sciences, is equally legitimate in the social sciences only by derivation: the generation of socio-technically applicable knowledge is a late by-product of a science that features a *practical-emancipatory* cognitive interest in its historical origin and its systematic possibilities. Arising in a situation of crisis in European civilization, sociology in its initial stages was (as Freyer in particular has shown[28]) a historically oriented "theory of the present age" with a practical intention —that is, with the purpose, supported by a practical concept of

28. H. Freyer, *Soziologie asls Wirklichkeitswissenschaft* (Leipzig and Berlin, 1930; Darmstadt, 1964).

progress, of overcoming the crisis in the sense of historical necessity and possibility; at the same time it was systematized written history. Hermeneutical theory has brought us to the point at which this explanation of sociology's original interest in cognition [29] enables us to see the direction of any search for a proficient integration of the until now still heterogeneous approaches of an interpretative and a causally explicative social science.

It has already been shown that explanatory sociology is always interpretative sociology as well; and that an interpretative sociology cannot be merely a subjective sociology of the interpretation of meaning. It is also clear now that the empirical content of social scientific theories is peculiarly proportional to the historical concretion to which they attain; and that, therefore, sociology is empirically substantial insofar as it allows its concepts concrete historical content. All this, however, is the result of the researcher's basic hermeneutical situation, and of the "obstinacy" of the socio-historical process which is his field of study; so that, finally, a claim to the sort of objectivity proper to physical science made by an historically oriented sociology is revealed as an objectivistic illusion, and social science is thrown back on its practical and emancipatory will to know. Habermas has tried to assess the consequences of this finding. Starting from a methodological consciousness that has exhausted itself in the contemporary forms of reflective knowledge, he attempts to renew critical theory as an empirical philosophy of history with a practical intention, or as an historically oriented social theory.[30] This is not the place for a systematic description of the methodological problems that such an undertaking has to face. I shall merely discuss two points which are extremely important for a basic understanding of Habermas's ideas, in order to tie

29. On the concept of an interest in cognition, see Jürgen Habermas, *Erkenntnis und Interesse* (Frankfurt, 1968), esp. section III, 9.

30. Cf., *inter al.*, *Erkenntnis und Interesse, Zur Logik der Sozialwissenschaften.*

them up with two questions that are more important for the present argument: that of the relationship of a revised critical theory with hermeneutics, and that of its relationship with Marx's theory.

The two points in question arise directly from the context that I have just discussed. One concerns the connection between explanation and interpretation in the context of a critical social theory that is practically and historically oriented; the other concerns the changed relationship between theory and practice (in regard to the natural sciences) which results from the dominance of a practical interest in cognition, and the new standards of measurement for verification and falsification that follow on that relationship.

Causal "explanation" in social science has already been recognized as always "interpretative." This, however, allows one to suspect that the original meaning of social scientific explanation is that of *interpretation* (in the sense of understanding) through explanation; that is, *explanatory understanding*.[31] From this viewpoint, the possibility of a still only socio-technical application of a purely legal or explicative knowledge would be the negative utopia *also* always contained in the process of men's scientific self-understanding of their socio-historical situation and the resulting practical imperative: because a society subjected to the pressures of nature and domination offers both points of vantage for a wholly technically objectifying theory, and positions of strength for a socio-technical application of that theory which will serve particular interests. But what, in contradistinction to this, is the meaning of an "explanatory interpretation"?

This meaning results from consideration of the possible significance of the aforesaid quasi-causal structures of social relations. These can represent objective significant relations which, precisely because they occur behind the backs of the behaving subjects, force these subjects to suffer an uncomprehended pressure that can be broken in thought and in practice only when

31. Cf. *Erkenntnis und Interesse,* section III, 11.

comprehended. Habermas has introduced the example of psychoanalysis in an attempt to clarify this point. The unconscious motives analyzed by Freud, which operate behind the active subject's back, have the practical local value of causes: "They are dispositions learned in frustration and conflict situations in early infancy. The behavior analyzed can therefore be described without reference to the fundamental motivation. Initially, only the psychoanalyst makes this reference. As soon as the interpretation of the patient's behavior (which at first exists only for the analyst) is avowed as correct by the patient himself, the unconscious motive can be resolved. Unconscious motives are so to speak disguised as causes; but only in this guise have they any motivating power." [32] If Habermas is right, in psychoanalysis the identification of behavioral dispositions that can be causally interpreted is the starting point for the reconstruction of an objective and intentional, social and life-historical context, the knowledge of which can break the spell of spontaneously effective, repressively produced pressures. But then psychoanalysis, which seeks to apply typical socialization processes with the aid of a general interpretative framework, is an explanatory theory with the practical aim of making developmental processes which have taken a pathological course *intelligible* and consequently curable. Of course, it is impossible to generalize on the basis of this model pure and simple. Nevertheless it serves to show that the recognition of quasi-causal regularities can permit the reconstruction of significant contexts which, because they are established without the knowledge of the subjects in question, exert a power that can be broken in practice only through comprehension.

Already apparent is the changed relation of theory and practice that exists for a critical social theory derived from a practical interest in cognition. Critical theory is derivable from a notion of the "good life" already available to it as part of the socio-

32. *Zur Logik der Sozialwissenschaften*, p. 186. Cf. *Erkenntnis und Interesse*, section III, 11 and 12.

historical situation it subjects to analysis; which, as the notion of an acknowledgement of each individual as a person by every other individual, and as the idea of a non-coercive communal human life of dialogue, is a draft meaning of history already fragmentarily embodied in a society's traditions and institutions: a draft meaning which it applies critically in opposing a society and its dominant forms of self-understanding. By concretizing this meaning of history as an outline of the objectively necessary and possible next step, and in certain negation of existing social un-freedom, critical theory is subjected to a double standard of measurement: it *exists* only by virtue of the reflective recognition of those "who speak and act for it," and it can *prove* itself only in successful social practice which erodes a fraction of actual constraint. In other words: the diagnosis that it offers to society, and its outline of future practice, can prove themselves ultimately only in the free acknowledgement of those men who have experienced as real freedom an alteration of society deriving from this theory. When hermeneutical thought has finally destroyed the historico-philosophical objectivism of the older theories, critical theory must avow its hypothetical status: it conceives itself as part of an experimental historical *praxis,* whose criterion of success is successful emancipation itself. Of course, this does not mean that in doing this it despises the recognized criteria of success of the empirico-analytical sciences, where their theorems, in accordance with their own claim, *have to* acknowledge these criteria of success; it merely means that critical theory repudiates the claim to objectivity put forward by the empirico-analytical sciences where it *actually* avails itself of the objectivity produced only in the dimension of social practice.

4.

The apparently straightforward convergence of critical theory and hermeneutics suggested by the argument up to this point conceals a problem the significance of which became clear in

41

the course of the controversy between Gadamer and Habermas. Until now I have tacitly accepted the validity of Gadamer's standpoint, namely, that a radicalized form of hermeneutical thought had previously entered Habermas's criticism of the claim to universality on the part of hermeneutical method, and that this hermeneutical thought must now put in question any further claims advanced by critical theory. Gadamer's position, which —in this regard—might perhaps be summarized as maintaining that "historically effective consciousness [. . .] is unavoidably more a matter of *being* than of *being conscious,*"[33] is, I think, consistent. Nevertheless, it does not seem to touch on the essential question of specific prejudices attaching to a hermeneutical consciousness unilaterally oriented to the human sciences (*Geisteswissenschaften*). I would say that a bias of this kind also determines the way in which Gadamer defends the universalist claim (or, perhaps one should say, the meta-theoretical status) of hermeneutics vis-à-vis the claims of critical theory.

I should now like to refer to Gadamer's reconstruction of the prehistory of Romantic hermeneutics in *Wahrheit und Methode* (*Truth and Method*).[34] This reconstruction shows clearly that the attenuations of the concept of understanding (*Verstehen*), which made it the central concept of nineteenth-century hermeneutics and which depend on a methodical factoring out of the problem of truth, result from the diminution of authority of the Christian and classical traditions, that until then had enjoyed a canonical status. Gadamer uses Spinoza to illustrate this point: for Spinoza, according to the norms of enlightened reason the *incomprehensible* content of the Bible which provokes hermeneutical thought is at one and the same time its *unreasonable content; consequently,* an *historical* interpretation on the basis of the intellect, situation and prejudices of the

33. Gadamer, *op. cit.,* p. 127.
34. Cf. Gadamer, *Wahrheit und Methode* (Tübingen, 1960), pp. 162 ff.

author is called for.[35] In this way the unreasonable is made historically comprehensible. What is interesting in the transition to Romantic hermeneutics (as Gadamer has pointed out [36]) is that the "incomprehensibility" of texts has a quite different significance for Schleiermacher. It might be said that Spinoza works on the basis of a secondary context of tradition, namely, the critical tradition of modern empirical science; hence he is forced to view the loss of authority of ecclesiastical tradition as the revelation of its untrue content: the incomprehensible is the unreasonable. For Schleiermacher, on the other hand, this equation is cancelled and with it the connection between hermeneutical thought and criticism: "misunderstanding" as a universal problem, as a structural danger to understanding *in general,* no longer indicates an "agreement" with tradition impeded by loss of authority, emancipation and criticism, but the irremovable reciprocal alienation of individuals seeking to come to an understanding with one another. This universalization of hermeneutics, which also causes the concern with understanding to discard its negative reference to the truth problem, enables it on the one hand to be pressed into the service of the restoration of demoted authority (Schleiermacher), but marks out for it on the other hand the path towards the fulfillment of the Enlightenment in a consciousness of history.

The questions that arise now are: (1) What is the significance (in regard to these attenuations of hermeneutical consciousness) of the attempt of a radicalized hermeneutical theory to make effective the principle of history-in-operation? (2) What is the significance of the rehabilitation of tradition, prejudice and authority, in view of their discrediting by the Enlightenment? These two questions must be resolved differently, according to whether the answer comes from the enlightened historical consciousness, or from the belief in reason of the earlier phase of the Enlightenment. The hermeneutical criticism of historical consciousness is

35. *Ibid.*, pp. 169 ff.
36. *Ibid.*, pp. 172 ff.

43

primarily the criticism of an objectivistic illusion: as such it has already been taken into account in my foregoing remarks on methodology, from which it should be clear, too, why hermeneutical criticism cannot enter into a critique of hermeneutics. But what about the hermeneutical criticism of the Enlightenment belief in reason?

Gadamer's criticism seems to me to rely on a peculiar reduction of the problem that is not uncharacteristic of the German tradition. In question here are the "dogmatic presuppositions" of the Enlightenment. In Gadamer's critique the prejudices of the historical consciousness appear as the most extreme consequences of these dogmatic presuppositions; the direction of the critique is determined from this basis. Hence the difference between the older form of biblical hermeneutics and the Bible criticism of the Enlightenment can be interpreted as a difference in the dogmatic basis of exegesis; Gadamer uses the case of Spinoza to show how, in place of the dogmatic principles of exegesis laid down by ecclesiastical tradition, the belief in reason itself becomes the dogmatic foundation of biblical exegesis.[37] In fact this belief in reason shows itself to be *dogmatic* from the viewpoint of hermeneutical criticism: subjective reason augments its force from that very context of tradition which it opposes abstractly in an "anti-authoritarian guise." At first all that this goes to show is that a self-conception of the Enlightenment is dogmatic, but not that the course of the Enlightenment is to be measured solely by this dogmatic self-misconception and its practical results. Without wishing to insinuate that Gadamer does precisely this, it seems possible that his rehabilitation of tradition, prejudice and authority is not a just account of the total contribution of the Enlightenment in this regard.

In referring to Gadamer's presentation of Spinoza's Bible criticism I tried to free it from the abstract Enlightenment antithesis of reason and authority by drawing attention to a "secondary" context of tradition, which was, in fact, the sole source

37. *Ibid.*, p. 170.

from which Enlightenment reason could derive its authority. Seen in this context, the "incomprehensible content" of Christian tradition is represented as the "unreasonable content" of ecclesiastical tradition and its claim to the belief and obedience of men as against another tradition: that of modern empirical science and the accompanying changes in practical social life. The theory and practice of this new context of tradition produced experiences and attitudes which put the officially sanctioned forms of the development of tradition in question in an increasingly radical fashion. The context of tradition as a whole became a theoretical and practical struggle between critical and dogmatic forms of the development of tradition. Just as here the terms "critical" and "dogmatic" cannot be emptied of reference to inherited forms of domination, so the critical principle of the Enlightenment cannot be freed from the same reference; in contradistinction to the dogmatic self-conception of the Enlightenment, it may be formulated as the principle that no inherited authority which *contradicts* reasoned understanding has any claim to the belief and obedience of men. This principle is revolutionary because it secures reason as an ability and demand of men themselves: this is the truth-component of the Enlightenment's dogmatic belief in reason. I find it significant that where the Enlightenment traditions have been more continuously effective than in Germany, criticism of this dogmatic belief in reason and of rationalistic and empiricist causal theory is able to make finer distinctions than hermeneutical criticism between the critical intentions of the Enlightenment and its dogmatic self-misconception: Peirce and Popper (each in his own way) have rehabilitated tradition and prejudice; but, with Popper in particular, this rehabilitation is accompanied by a universal critical approach relying on a general rejection of causal theory. Even though the universalist approach of this form of criticism makes it problematical, it contains a hermeneutical insight which hermeneutics treats with extraordinary reserve, namely, that every claim to truth on the part of tradition contains the promise of

45

future verification, and therefore must ultimately be measured against its fulfillment and method of fulfillment of this promise; and that *understanding* (interpretation), on which hermeneutics depends, occurs (and is required) precisely in the case of a promise that is not fulfilled. However, this shows the close connection between hermeneutic effort and criticism. Despite its origin in the experience of a loss of traditional authority, in the hermeneutics of the human sciences (*Geisteswissenschaften*)— as a result of their particular modifications of the concept of understanding—, this relationship occurs only in an attenuated form: as the relationship (resulting from the hermeneutic circle in the more restricted sense) between the understanding of contexts of meaning (texts) and the rectification of an individual prejudice, in which the critical instance is unilaterally impregnated with the "dominant force" of tradition to which the hermeneutical effort is directed.[38] Gadamer's rehabilitation of tradition, prejudice and authority, it seems to me, strangely ignores this (now perhaps really methodically necessary) "professional deformation" of "normal" hermeneutic consciousness;[39] precisely this feature of his work would seem to lay bare the remarkably ambivalent nature of his universalization of hermeneutics.

However that may be, it brings us to the decisive point. The Enlightenment consciousness viewed the experience of a loss of authority on the part of traditions as the experience of force: that is, the experience of a *claim* to authority which, insofar as it did not meet with voluntary acknowledgement, was able to gain currency only by coercion. Consequently, the Enlightenment principle of reason can be interpreted as the demand for the abrogation of all repressive conditions that could claim no legitimacy other than their sheer existence; reason not as a

38. *Ibid.,* p. 295.
39. This can, I think, be seen from the way in which Gadamer tries to place cultural *and* historical hermeneutics in terms of theological and legal hermeneutics. Cf. *op. cit.,* pp. 294 ff.

counter-concept to authority, but as the principle of voluntary communication in contrast to the experienced actuality of a process of communication distorted by violence. The course of the Enlightenment as an extension of Western Christian tradition reveals what might be called its "revolutionary core": the intention to achieve actual freedom in view of the inherited lack of freedom in practice; the spirit of criticism in view of the equally inherited legitimations of a lack of freedom. This tendency of the Enlightenment cannot be separated from the political movements for emancipation in modern times; this connection, however, emphasizes what the Enlightenment knew and hermeneutics forgets: that the "dialogue" which (according to Gadamer) we "are," is *also* a relationship of coercion and, for this very reason, *no* dialogue at all.

The fact that the relation of hermeneutics to the Enlightenment has remained essentially ambivalent can certainly be ascribed to the methodical attenuations which made a hermeneutical consciousness possible in the first place. On the one hand, the operative historical consciousness elevates historical consciousness as the extreme consequence of the Enlightenment consciousness in itself; on the other hand, it cannot at the same time make allowance for historical consciousness falling behind the Enlightenment, and therefore shares the latter's negative attitude to the Enlightenment. This is the source of that conservative trait which, Habermas says, always enables "us to justify a dangerous claim to superiority and has separated us from Western traditions." [40]

Consequently, the universalist claim of the hermeneutical approach can be upheld only if one assumes that, as the location of possible truth and factual comprehension, the context of tradition is at one and the same time the location of factual untruth and permanent coercion. This is an insight of the Enlightenment (not of critical theory) as little open to dissolution by hermeneutics as it is to full realization by a critical theory.

40. Habermas, *Zur Logik der Sozialwissenschaften*, p. 176.

Nevertheless, critical theory does attempt to follow the implications of this insight in trying to reconstruct the context of tradition *as* a context of work and coercion; or, in Marxist terms, as the dialectics of the productive forces and the conditions of production. This reconstruction of history is also the reconstruction of an objective context of meaning—of one that, of course could enter human consciousness only *in this form* as a result of the revolutionary upheavals since the end of the eighteenth century. This reconstruction of history is subordinate to an interest in an historical reconstruction of modern social conditions as a *criticism* of these conditions; that is: the sort of understanding it aims at is an historical understanding of the relations of domination experienced *as* coercion, and of the legitimations of domination comprehended in advance as untrue, for the purpose of their critical dissolution. The claim of critical theory to be able to perceive a still effective self-understanding of society, as it were "from the wings", admittedly depends on immanent criticism taking effect simultaneously: it is the famed *topos* of the "contradictions" of the total context of social life, in which this "hermeneutical" insight into the determining factors and limits of the criticism of ideology has always been latent. These contradictions of the historical context of tradition, expressed in criticism and coercion, are the very factors which hermeneutical method has always failed to take into account.

What are the implications for the relationship between critical theory and hermeneutics? The interest in emancipation, which actuates critical theory, can be provoked only by the experience of repression and suffering—or, in Habermas's terms, by the experience of distorted communication; as an interest in knowledge it is also an interest in practical emancipation. But this also means that critical theory can initiate a critical and practical dissolution of inherited and historically redundant conditions of coercion (a dissolution resulting *from* and *in* enlightenment) only if it is in a position to make an historically

48

effective interest in liberation aware of its own nature. The idea must not only take hold of the masses in order to become material force; it must become the idea *of* the enlightened masses, so that the force they exert can be enlightened practice. This is the actual starting point of the difficulties of critical theory: that is, its specific risks, dilemmas, and illusions. Just as the critical and practical dissolution of institutionalized coercive relations is bound up with an historically concrete "materialization" of the emancipation-interests in the repressed sector of society, so the specific articulation of this interest (and at the same time the definition of practical goals) remains enclosed in the pathologically distorted social context of communication. At this point it is necessary to apply the hermeneutical reservation that the operative historical consciousness is inevitably more "being" than "being conscious." Insofar as the idea of freedom becomes the guiding concept of an emancipatory criticism, it remains a problematical "prejudice." This means on the one hand that criticism as science can be made cogent and imperative only when joined with successful liberating practice. Only a new state of things—freedom actually experienced—can confirm the anticipation of possible freedom and make it universally acknowledged. This means on the other hand that the degeneration of a *praxis* based on emancipatory criticism must remain a structural danger of emancipatory practice, as long as this practice can take place only under the conditions of distorted communication (that is, continuous pressures of nature and domination), and therefore remains open to the danger of ideological self-delusion. As unfree men we possess the concept of freedom and the good life, yet we are not its masters: this is a dilemma that critical theory, unaware as yet of the future of its own practice, has to face.

But how about the other side of the balance-sheet? Because critical theory tries to reveal and illuminate the history, conditions, and significance of that "dialogue" which, according to hermeneutics, we "are," and which for hermeneutics must re-

49

main *qua* reflection an ultimate datum; and because critical theory tries especially to delineate the history of the distortions of this "dialogue" (a history about which hermeneutics by itself can offer no information), it has for its part to challenge the universalist claim of the hermeneutical approach, as expressed in an hermeneutical ontology. This means first of all that critical theory undertakes an *extension* of hermeneutical thought. The effort of "understanding" (*Verstehen*), in contrast to traditional hermeneutics up to Gadamer, achieves a new dimension; not only when, instance by instance, the distortion of the historical context of human communication is taken into account as a fact, but when the question of the meaning and the coercive logic of such distortions is brought to the mid-point of the discussion. Systematically, this problem can be resolved only by means of a critical reconstruction of the history of a human species laboring under the pressures of nature and domination, and simultaneously constituting itself *in* them. Together with Habermas,[41] I would give the following provisional account of this reconstruction of history: It starts from the conflict arising from the natural basis of human history—the fundamental conflict between the conditions of collective survival and the particular historical overflows of dynamic potential; and is based on the immanent logic of men's progressive technological self-objectification.[42] It tries then to reveal the functional and dysfunctional links between the development of the forces of production and forms of domination. In association with a critical theory of modern society, this reconstruction of history provides the key for an understanding—*as criticism*—of tradition insofar as we recover ourselves in it—but *not* as in a "dialogue." Interest in this kind of understanding is not sim-

41. Cf., especially, Habermas, *Erkenntnis und Interesse* (Frankfurt, 1968), Section 12; also his *Technik und Wissenschaft als "Ideologie"* (Frankfurt, 1968).

42. Cf., on this point, A. Gehlen, "Anthropologische Ansicht der Technik," in Freyer *et al.* (eds.), *Technik im technischen Zeitalter* (Düsseldorf, 1965), as well as the references supplied there.

50

EMPIRICO-ANALYTICAL AND CRITICAL SOCIAL SCIENCE

ply interest in understanding pure and simple, but the more
fundamental form of interest in emancipation from the conditions of coercion, which are experienced as failure and alienation and can be criticized as historically superfluous. This kind
of comprehension of tradition *against* tradition is therefore in
itself a partial emancipation *from* tradition, insofar as the latter
is a coercive relationship, and at the same time the precondition of emancipation in practice. As criticism, it is possible
only in the shape of science, for only science can lay open the
ideological contents of cultural traditions, so to speak, from
outside the context of tradition.

This does not mean that the hermeneutical reservations have
to be retracted again, but merely that the standpoint of finite-
nesss is invoked *against* hermeneutics by bringing into consideration the finite determinations of the context of tradition
hypostatized by hermeneutics. It means that the possibility of
a sublating self-transcendence of the context of tradition in
consciousness and in practice is made apparent, without a repeated infusion of all those hypostatizations that have weighed
down the post-Hegelian-Marxist tradition.

Hermeneutical criticism has demonstrated that critical theory
cannot lay claim to the status of a meta-theory in regard to
hermeneutics. Without committing myself to the hazardous assertion that critical theory has already *proved* the converse to
be true of hermeneutics, nevertheless such a reversal of the critique seems to be both necessary and justified: it would mean
the destruction of hermeneutics as an ontology. But for the
time being the judicial circumstances and counter-pleas of this
time-honored suit do not seem wholly clear, so the verdict must
remain open.

5.

Habermas's approach to an empirical philosophy of history
with a practical purpose is a highly serious attempt to renew

critical theory on the level of a modern conception of method-ology. Consequently, critical theory sees the tiresome procedure of a study of the methodological self-representation of modern science as a necessity, because it has been profoundly shaken by a double forfeiture of practice: by its dogmatic ossification in the socialist countries of the East with their authoritarian and bureaucratic régimes, and by its involution as a culture-critical philosophy in the capitalist societies of the West. In both forms it has not only practically forfeited its place in the acknowledged canon of the sciences, but has to a considerable extent sur-rendered what, in accordance with its original intention, is its decisive function: the self-consciousness of a political struggle for the emancipation of mankind from the total coercive con-text of its history to date.

The early Horkheimer's opposition to bourgeois science was also, as part of an actual political conflict, a struggle *against* this science: with a proletariat ready for battle and the wind of history bringing up the rearguard. Even if Horkheimer did not labor under any too great illusions regarding the degree of awareness of the proletariat of his time, he was still able—for good reasons—to incorporate it as a revolutionary force in his historico-philosophical estimate. Consequently, in contrast to a bureaucratically ossified socialism and to bourgeois science, he was able still to place his hopes entirely on a (so to speak) purely dialectical restoration of the basic Marx. His hopes were not borne out. The later extensions of critical theory by Adorno, Horkheimer and Marcuse therefore include a tacit avowal of the absence of any reference to *praxis*: critical theory conceives itself as a protest, but as a protest impotent in practice, against an apocalyptically self-obturating system of alienation and reifi-cation; and as the spark whose preservation in a self-darkening world will keep alive the memory of something quite different. The eventual irruption of this "something else" became the object of a hope that grew in wisdom but at the same time was touched with despair in the process of trying to make it out.

Adorno's musical and literary-critical essays are fascinating in the extreme as documentation of this phase of critical theory; at the same time they are unmistakable evidence of its precarious double isolation: in the context of the sciences, *and* in that of politics.

Habermas tries to break through this twofold isolation of critical theory. Hence his original strategy, which is quite changed from that of the early Horkheimer. From the frustration of the revolutionary movements in Europe he deduces the need for a self-critical attitude on the part of critical theory, if it is to regain the lost relationship with political *praxis*. Critical theory can no longer merely assert its reliance on this relationship, but must first of all regain it in practice *and* in theory. Habermas's critical grappling with modern scientific theory therefore has a dual significance: on the one hand, it is a struggle for the critical soul of science; on the other, it is a struggle for the scientific soul of criticism—not in the sense of a concession to scientism's ideal of science, but assuredly in the sense of a concession to the anti-metaphysical and empiricist impulse of Anglo-American scientific theory, in which Habermas finds not just a flourishing ideology but at the same time—paradoxically enough—a certain extension of the Enlightenment tradition beyond Marx. Habermas's work is critical theory attempting, in a debate with analytical scientific theory and social science, to determine its critical position anew. It reveals the progressive and humane aspect of the anti-metaphysical and self-critical enthusiasm of "Science," and takes it into account: by means of a decisive elimination both of the metaphysical remnants in Marx's theory, and of the empirical contents of this theory that have congealed dogmatically in the Marxist tradition and have been overtaken historically. While accepting Marx in a critical spirit, it tries to go beyond him. Its intention is a revision of Marxism, starting from a changed historical situation and from a finite standpoint.

But this makes a critical examination of Marx's theory a

matter of immediate necessity. We must start from the assumption that the freezing of Marxism as a system of dogmatic metaphysics, already signalled in the history of the Second International, is no mere historical accident (cf. Landgrebe) which can be explained solely by, say, the frustration of the Russian Revolution—which was also the frustration of the European Revolution in general. Neither the pressure of unfavorable historical circumstances nor the lack of faith or of ability on the part of functionaries is an adequate excuse for the Stalinist and bureaucratic degeneration of socialist *praxis,* so long as one maintains that it is impossible to modify the theory that would be no more than the self-consciousness of this *praxis.* If not the nucleus then at least a theoretical correlative for the decline in practice must be available in the theory itself. There are two related aspects of theory in which, above all, the later decline of socialist theory and practice seems (in retrospect) to be announced: in a vestige of speculative thought in the interpretation of the revolutionary transition period, and of the associated eschatological supersession of the proletariat on the one hand, and in the role played by the concept of labor in Marx's theory of history and revolution, on the other. Here it is not a question of playing off the early against the later Marx, but rather the converse. But it is more probable, from the viewpoint chosen here, that the pertinent factor in the relationship of the late, "economic" Marx with the young "philosophical" Marx, is a transformation of the same speculative inheritance into another linguistic reference system.

In the *Introduction to a Critique of Hegel's Philosophy of Right,* Marx deduces the revolutionary role of the proletariat in all but philosophical terms (this has often been pointed out for critical ends); but, in itself, this still offers no argument against the theory of revolution held by the early Marx. For it accords with the essential purpose of Marx's critique of philosophy to use philosophy itself (or, more exactly, Hegelian philosophy imbued with real historical contents) in a confrontation with philosophy as such. Far more decisive is the fact that philosophic thought in the case of the early Marx has not yet assumed a really "unphilosophical" form; his critique of philosophy is not radical enough. In the world-historical "logicization" of the proletariat and its situation, in equipping it so to speak with the supernatural authority-*cum*-power and irresistible logic of absolute Spirit, there is even a trace of metaphysics. This logicization of the proletariat is clearly evident in the dialectical antitheses of the *Introduction,* especially when Marx describes the proletariat as the class of civil society, "which, in short, is the *total loss* of humanity, and can redeem itself only by the *total redemption* of humanity." [43] The *practical* necessity of the complete revolutionary emancipation of mankind by the proletariat—"in Germany the impossibility of gradual emancipation must produce complete freedom" [44]—is, by a mysterious twist of thought, seen at the same time as theoretical necessity. In *The Holy Family,* Marx speaks of "absolutely compelling need" as the "practical expression of necessity"; it is this need which not only *forces* the proletariat to act, but in the struggle for the bare necessities of life relentlessly drives it forward to its own emancipation. For: "It cannot free itself without transcending the conditions of its own life. It cannot transcend the conditions of its own life without transcending *all* inhuman conditions of present-day society, which are summed up in its own situation." [45] The necessity of the struggle, which results from extreme material need, converges with the practical necessity of emancipation, which arises from the connection between inhumanity and riches in existing society; from this convergence Marx deduces the necessity of the result, which is the necessity of an objective logic of history—not of the logic of finite human history, of course, but of that of absolute Spirit itself: "It is not

43. Karl Marx-Ausgabe, ed. H. J. Lieber, Vol. 1 (Darmstadt, 1962), p. 503. (This edition is hereafter referred to as MA.)
44. *Ibid.,* p. 503.
45. *Ibid.,* p. 705.

a matter of what this or that proletarian or even the whole proletariat *imagines* for the moment is the goal. It is a question of *what it* [the proletariat] *is,* and what in accordance with this *being* it is compelled to do historically. Its goal and its historical action are clearly and irrevocably marked out for it in its own life situation, as well as in the whole organization of present-day civil society." [46]

The argument up to this point cannot be taken as conclusive so long as the opposite account is not subjected to scrutiny. Marx's intention is not to outbid Hegel in the sense of making the proletariat the blind agent of an historical necessity which only the philosopher knows in advance. The proletariat is *neither* the blind agent of historical necessity *nor,* as self-conscious suffering, the direct consciousness of what is historically necessary; however, from this doubly negative determination Marx develops his most forceful ideas concerning the relationship between revolutionary theory and practice; for instance, when he says (in *The German Ideology*) that, "both for the production of this Communist consciousness on a mass scale, and for the success of the thing that really matters, an alteration of men on a mass scale is necessary, and this can occur only in a practical movement, in a *revolution;* hence this revolution is necessary, not only because the ruling class can be overthrown in no other way, but because only by a revolution can the class that overthrows it manage to rid itself of all the age-old trash, in order to become fitted to establish society anew." [47] The revolution itself is the formation-process of the revolutionary consciousness in which historical necessity is realized. The practical necessity of liberation in its full sense, as the overthrow of domination, can be turned from a necessity for the theoretician into a necessity for the masses only by means of the revolutionary struggle—this is an element of theory itself.

For Marx it is beyond question that in the process of the

46. *Ibid.,* p. 705.
47. *Ibid.,* p. 70.

self-production of free men through the revolutionary struggle of the proletariat, the positive results of history to date (civilization, humanization, the personalization of man) will be "transcended." That is: the emancipation of the proletariat actualizes the substantial freedom of all citizens that became a possibility with the development of the capitalist mode of production, and the concept of which has to date found only an ideological expression in philosophy; it is the realization of philosophy.

What basis has Marx for his belief that the consciousness of material need will have led, at the end of the revolutionary struggle, to a mass-scale perception of what is practically necessary, and hence to the success of the revolution? This trust can ultimately be explained only by Marx's tacit enfolding of the proletariat in the all too capacious cloak of the World Spirit, which *must* think and all at once realize what is reasonable—which is at the same time what is timely. For Marx the reasonable is always the real, for the logic of history—in accordance with which the proletariat strides ahead—is no longer seriously on probation; it guarantees in advance that the proletariat will only march in step with the World Spirit, but be wholly successful in its undertakings: "In any event, private property in its political economic movement is driven towards its own dissolution, but only by a development which does not depend on it, which takes place against its will but of which it is unconscious, and which is determined by the nature of things; only because it produces the proletariat *as* the proletariat—the spiritual and physical misery conscious of its misery, the alienation conscious of its dehumanization and hence transcending itself." [48]

In this pattern of thought in the early Marx, that believes the abrogation of alienation to be a necessary consequence of the abolition of capitalism based on private ownership, there is a vestige of historico-speculative objectivism that anticipates the élite voluntarism and Party dictatorship of later times. To

48. *Ibid.*, p. 704.

this extent, one must agree with Landgrebe when he establishes a connection between the metaphysical residue in Marx's theory and the *praxis* of the omniscient Party élite. The reasons Landgrebe gives for this, on the other hand, do not seem to me to fit the case. He writes: "Since Marx retained Hegel's conviction that it was possible to detect the goal of the history of this process of production, and that it must be the realization of universal liberation, but at the same time removed the foundation-stone from the Hegelian system, he deduced the following: History will not be taken forward to this goal by the exertion of divine power, the 'artifice of reason,' but (since this power does not exist) only through human action, the revolution of the proletariat. However, because man is aware of the law of history, he is able to determine the point at which the revolution will come about, and can therefore establish its strategy and tactics. Therefore he cannot remain satisfied with the assurance of the rule of a higher power in his reflective consideration of history, but *can offer forecasts of the future,* and must himself act according to these prognostications. But it follows that those who understand the law of history and know how to apply it can require absolute obedience in regard to what-must-be-done in accordance with this knowledge. This is the *basis of a demand for absolute obedience between man and man, which becomes imperative if absolute knowledge no longer has the validity of the reflection of divine reason, but only that of human understanding.* For there is no longer any power on whose commandment men can rely in their resistance to human commands. But then the requirement of the freedom of all is no longer justifiable as a claim of men *qua* men. *By removing from Hegel's philosophy the foundation-stone supporting the demand for the recognition of the freedom of men qua men, and at the same time retaining Hegel's conviction that history is oriented to the realization of the freedom of all men, and to the abrogation of all repression of men by men, Marx has removed the basis of*

58

his conviction and, contrary to his own intention, has prepared the ground for the possibility of totalitarian domination." [49]

If I understand it correctly, Landgrebe's argument runs as follows: Marx is no longer able to follow Hegel in interpreting the idea of a necessary liberation of all men as the reflection of a divine revelation, but has to give it a basis in man himself. Consequently, however, he is compelled to devalue the idea, in the sense of an ideology allied to specific conditions of production. Therefore, by removing the divine origin of the goal of history developed by Hegel in the process of speculative thought (that is, the goal of the abrogation of the repression of men by men, the acknowledgement of all by all), he simultaneously removes the premiss "which alone allows affirmation of the dignity of man as a free, historically effective being" (p. 63). "Therefore the assertion of the scientific possibility of the recognition of the goal of history and the way to it is now based on an absolute knowledge, that is not the reflection of the idea of divine revelation, but is available to man as the absolute master of his own destiny, as being himself the supreme being. But when it becomes clear that this assertion requires the simultaneous removal of the premisses that allow it meaning in the first place, the result is that this claim to the scientific ascertainability of the way leading to the goal of history has to be relinquished." [50]

Landgrebe is justified in stressing the contradiction between the concept of a meaning of history produced by man himself and the objectivistic claim to scientific ascertainability of the goal of history and the way leading to this goal. I have already characterized this objectivism as *historico-speculative* objectivism, and asserted that it indicates a vestige of metaphysics in Marx's thought that runs contrary to his essential intentions. In contrast to Landgrebe's finding, therefore, it has to be shown

49. L. Landgrebe, "Das Problem der Dialektik," in *Marxismusstudien* III (Tübingen, 1960), p. 63.
50. *Ibid.,* p. 64.

that the "scientific status" of Marx's theory can and must be understood *in such a way* that it does not include the precise variety of objectivism that Landgrebe finds in it, without this meaning that the theory itself must surrender its fundamental content. In short, proof is needed that Marx's theory obtains its potential precisely from its understanding of the "meaning of history" as a product of human history itself.

I shall attempt to demonstrate this in two stages. In the second stage I shall revert to the criticism of the role of the concept of labor in Marx's theory, from which (as Habermas has shown) it is possible to perceive Marx's vagueness about the notion of science that he implicitly relies on.

1. The precise point of Marx's critique of religion is, I think, that he not only conceived man as the true and unique subject of history, but simultaneously revealed in the ideological forms of conciliation—religion and philosophy—the human outlines of a *real* conciliation hidden in the protest against actual misery, thereby disclosing the human outline of a meaning of history. This meaning of history, which is possibly grounded in an interest (with roots going far back into human anthropology) in a mutual human communication no longer distorted by the pressures of nature and human domination, is initially something already met with in tradition—a meaning already incorporated in and recognized in social institutions, though in a distorted and ideological form. Precisely because this meaning is no longer guaranteed by a divine court of appeal, and precisely because men, as the creators of history, are at one and the same time the creators of its meaning, this meaning can be grasped in reality only as a practical human task. The criticism of ideology therefore also implies that the meaning of history recognized by men can be grasped in its true significance only as a practical task. At the same time Marx recognizes the necessity of the ideological illusion of an (only apparent) reconciliation under historical circumstances, in which, on account of the scarcity of food and the inferior state of the forces of production, domi-

nation and exploitation had to recur continually. This exploitation of man by man has become most marked in capitalist society; at the same time, however, it has produced both the social wealth which makes exploitation superfluous, and the impoverished masses who must revolt against this exploitation: this is the historic moment of truth in which a "meaning" of history can and must be grasped as a practical task: "The self-consciously acting proletariat affirms at one and the same time the meaning of history to date and their own historical action, which alone fulfills this meaning because it realizes it." [51]

The moral physiognomy of capitalist society has been analyzed on innumerable occasions since Marx: not least in the major contributions of the later Frankfurt School, which already start from the assumption that the "misery and horror" can still be experienced in actuality only on the margins and in the upheavals of this society. When Marx deduced this moral countenance from the innermost structure of capitalist society, he was wholly uncontaminated by any trace of metaphysics in seeing the abrogation of private capital ownership as the inevitable prerequisite for the emancipation of men from the misery for which they themselves were responsible, and therefore for a realization of the meaning of history. Of course the early Marx at least was aware of the practical necessity and objective possibility of this step, when still under the sway of Hegel's world-historical logic, and aware of it, too, as the realization and "fulfilment" of the meaning of history. Ultimately, of course, for Marx the human revolution would mature in accordance with a superhuman logic. Only by forgoing the contingency of a human undertaking threatened by frustration and expiry in a finite situation, was it possible for that objectivistic illusion to appear in theory, whose far-distant reflection Landgrebe detects in the Stalinist terror. I would summarize my response to Landgrebe's assertion as follows: Marx cannot be accused of "vestigial metaphysics" in deriving from Hegel a meaning of

51. Iring Fetscher, *Marxismusstudien* II (Tübingen, 1957), p. 39.

history which would be meaningless when stripped of its divine origin, but in comprehending the action of the proletariat which transcends the historical situation by means of revolution, simultaneously as the ultimate action of Absolute Spirit. Marx produced only a half-hearted extra-Hegelian secularization of Christian eschatology: beneath his image of the suffering proletariat there is still the authoritative power of God, which guarantees salvation.

Of course all this holds true, properly speaking, only for the early Marx. The suprahuman logic of history, which, as I have already maintained, guaranteed for the early Marx the fulfillment of feedom in the proletarian revolution, has a wholly human face in the later works: it is the logic of human labor—which brings me to the second stage of the promised demonstration.

2. From here on I shall refer to observations of Habermas, to be found mainly in two of his more recent works; [52] here too, I shall have to reproduce only the bare outline of the argument. In his contribution to a *Festschrift* for Karl Löwith, Habermas tried to show that the mature Hegelian system arose from the modification of an approach developed by Hegel in the Jena *Philosophy of the Spirit*. In short, Habermas's thesis is that, for the Jena Hegel (in contrast to the Hegel of the *Encyclopaedia*), language, work and communicative behavior are three equally original basic dialectical models in the process of formation of spirit (mind), which cannot be reduced to one another even though they are mutually interwoven. They are also three different basic models of the dialectical relationship between subject and object, which combine to produce "the developed identity of the naming, subtle and recognized consciousness." [53] But

52. "Arbeit und Interaktion," in H. Plessner (ed.), *Natur und Geschichte* (Festschrift for Karl Löwith; Stuttgart, 1967); *Erkenntnis und Interesse* (Frankfurt, 1968).
53. *Arbeit und Interaktion,* p. 142.

the dialectics of work and that of communicative behavior, in particular, are not subject to reduction to one another; the one is synonymous with the "process of alienation (reification) and appropriation," and the other, as the "dialectics of love and war," with the process of dissension and reconciliation.[54] For reasons grounded in the idealistic premiss of the thesis of identity, the later Hegel (this is Habermas's suggestion) synchronized the three initially heterogeneous dialectical models[55]: so that in the *Encyclopaedia*," language and work, formerly structural models for the movement of the dialectic," become "subordinate real circumstances." [56]

This is why Marx, in his later materialistic transformation of Hegel, was able to interpret the dialectical process of the self-production of the human species unilaterally, that is, from the viewpoint of *work*: "The major achievement of Hegel's *Phenomenology* and its end-result [. . .] is that Hegel conceives the self-production of man as a process, objectification as loss of the object, as alienation and transcendence of this alienation, and that, consequently, he conceives the nature of work and comprehends the objective, true because real man, as the result of his own labor." [57] Marx's insight into the dialectical relation between productive forces and conditions of production—forms of work, and stages in power of technical control of natural processes on the one hand, and forms of socialization on the other hand—could be easily misinterpreted in a mechanistic fashion, because he does not really develop fully his exposition of dialectics: Marx's theory is controlled by a form of systematics in which interaction is ultimately reduced to labor, while productive work becomes a "paradigm for the generation of all categories." [58] Habermas has recently thor-

54. *Ibid.*, p. 149.
55. *Ibid.*, pp. 148 ff.
56. *Ibid.*, p. 147.
57. *Economic and Philosophical Manuscripts*, in MA, Vol. 1, p. 645.
58. Cf. Habermas, *op. cit.*, p. 153.

oughly demonstrated this thesis, and the implications for a critique of Marx's concept of science. As a working hypothesis, this thesis shows that the metaphysical remnant in Marx's theory is also a remnant of positivism: hence the critique of analytical theory by critical theory would ultimately become self-criticism.

If it is basically true that productive work, for Marx, becomes paradigmatic for the generation of all categories, that is, if he tacitly conceives the revolutionary "production" of the realm of freedom according to the pattern of instrumental or strategic action, then at least we would have found an intellectual-historic (*geistesgeschichtlich*) origin for the technocratic corruption of socialism: the authoritarian and bureaucratic organization of social un-freedom as the caricature of the realm of freedom would probably be based on latent features of Marx's own theory. Then one would have to examine the political ethics of Stalinism from this viewpoint: a political strategy in which the end justifies the means, is conceived according to the model of the technical control of natural processes on the lines of an ends-rationalization—a model in which means and ends are related arbitrarily and superficially. When this model becomes the fundamental pattern of socialist strategy, rationality becomes force, and the realm of freedom can only be an extreme form of the domination of men by men.

Similarly, the nature or self-conception of Marxist theory cannot be unaffected if Marx really understood work to be the paradigm for social *praxis* pure and simple. For the relationship of theory and practice existing between the empirico-analytical sciences and their technical application applies in the sphere of labor. The application of the theory is external to its validity; the theory merely offers reliable conditional prognoses which, as the ends demand in each particular case, can be converted into successful instrumental action. The empirico-analytical sciences, in particular the natural sciences, can be directly conceived as the paradigm and developed form of the knowledge obtained in the cognitive-anthropological reference-system of instrumental behavior, in which nature constitutes "existence subject to laws." From this angle, it no longer seems accidental that Marx oriented his concept of science by that of the natural sciences, whose direct connection with "industry" he demonstrated so strikingly. If "work," for Marx, is the basic category of the philosophy of history and the anthropology of cognition, then the objectivistic illusion of natural scientific theories must redound upon his own historical and social theory. Consequently, the position of the concept of work in Marx's theory would be the focal point to which can be traced the conversion of the dialectical logic of history of Absolute Spirit into the developmental mechanics of vulgar Marxism. Contrary to his declared intentions, Marx would then have had a share in both.

2. THE LATENT POSITIVISM OF MARX'S PHILOSOPHY OF HISTORY

1.

My critique of the objectivism of Marx's philosophy of history was directed at a latently positivistic misconception, which, according to Habermas's thesis, arises from the part played in Marx's theory by the concept of labor. Of course it would be a basic misunderstanding of this thesis to suppose that Habermas's concept of "instrumental behavior" could conceal Marx's notion of production. It is well-known that when Marx talks of "production" in his economic analyses, he also means "distribution," "forms of intercourse"—which corresponds to "communicative behavior." [1] Habermas also makes a distinction between the level of material analyses, on which Marx makes use of a concept of social practice incorporating labor *and* interaction,[2] and the level of historico-philosophical interpretation, on which Marx comprehends the self-production (that is, creation) of the human species solely on the basis of the logic of its activity in the production of objects: "For his analysis of the development of socio-economic formations Marx uses a concept of the system of social labor containing more elements than are declared in the concept of the self-creating human species. Self-constitution through social work is conceived *on the categorical*

1. Cf. Marx, *Grundrisse der Kritik der politischen Ökonomie* (Berlin, 1953), Introduction, pp. 16 ff.
2. Cf. Jürgen Habermas, *Erkenntnis und Interesse*, p. 71.

level as a production process; and instrumental behavior, work in the sense of productive activity, characterizes the dimension in which natural history runs its course. *On the level of his material investigations,* on the other hand, Marx always takes into account a social *praxis* incorporating work *and* interaction; the natural-historical processes are intermediated by the productive activity of the individual and the organization of its intercourse." [3] The epistemological implications of Marx's understanding of history lead to the misconception of ideology-critical social theory as a "science" in the same sense as the natural sciences, which Marx in fact favored.[4] The camouflaging of the difference between "strict experimental science" and "criticism," [5] between "productive knowledge" and reflective knowledge," would necessarily have consequences in regard to the apprehension of the interplay of critical theory and revolu-

3. *Ibid.,* p. 71.
4. In his Preface to the second edition of *Capital* (Vol. I), for example, Marx quotes (with approval) a Russian reviewer who compares Marx's method of economic analysis with a biology oriented to the history of evolution: "Marx views the social movement as a process of natural history, governed by laws which are not only independent of the will, consciousness and intelligence of men, but on the contrary determine their volition, consciousness and intelligence" (MA, Vol. 4, p. xxix). Marx acknowledges the reviewer's description as a representation of his dialectical *method* (*ibid.,* p. xxx); this is fatal in view of the following, far-reaching assertion by the reviewer: "Consequently, Marx is concerned with only one thing: to show, by precise scientific investigation, the necessity of successive definite systems of social conditions, and to establish, as impartially as possible, the facts that serve him as starting points and grounds. For this purpose it is wholly adequate if he proves, at one and the same time, the necessity of the present order and the necessity of another order into which the first must inevitably pass over, quite oblivious of whether men believe or do not believe it, are conscious or unconscious of it" (*ibid.,* p. xxix). These statements already show that a positivistic self-misconception cannot fail to affect even the material contents of the theory—here in particular the interpretation of the world-historical transition to the classless society. Subsequently, I try to demonstrate the inner context of theory that allowed Marx—not quite by accident—to let pass these statements by his St. Petersburg reviewer.
5. Cf. *Erkenntnis und Interesse, op. cit.,* p. 62.

tionary practice: Marx's self-conception provides the starting points for an erroneously technocratic interpretation of his theory, which was then to become practical reality in the hands of the omniscient administrators of historical necessity.[6]

Of course the two levels of material analysis and categorical interpretation are not related as object- and meta-level. The categorical framework already includes an historico-philosophical articulation which allows the production of basic statements about the "mechanism" of historical development. These pronouncements however have, as it were, no merely meta-theoretical status;[7] consequently, one might suppose that the contradiction between theory *qua* criticism and its objectivistic self-misconception has an inner-theoretical correlative in the form of a contradiction between the historical interpretation of historical materialism and the criticism of political economy. Of course this supposition, formulated in this global way, is *prima facie* implausible: historical materialism enters into the approach proper to the criticism of political economy, just as much as it is the result of that approach.[8]

In addition, the criticism of political economy becomes a *criticism of ideology,* inasmuch as it turns into what Lukács calls an "historical criticism of economy."[9] When Marx criticizes

---

6. Cf. Oskar Negt, Introduction to A. Deborin and N. Bukharin, *Kontroversen über dialektischen und mechanistischen Materialismus* (Frankfurt, 1969).

7. Otherwise one would only need to disengage Marx's statements about the scientific status of his theory and his "meta-theory" of history from the body of the theory, and to allow them to speak for themselves as against their positivistic misinterpretations. It should soon become apparent that the matter is more complex than this.

8. For the first part of the assertion cf. K. Marx, *Grundrisse der Kritik der politischen Ökonomie* (Berlin, 1953), Introduction, esp. sections 2 and 3. The most effective evidence for the second part is the connection between the beginning and the end of *Capital;* cf. K. Kosik, *Dialektik des Konkreten* (Frankfurt, 1967), pp. 174 ff.

9. Cf. Georg Lukács, "Klassenbewusstsein," in *Geschichte und Klassenbewusstsein* (Amsterdam, 1967), p. 60.

commodity-fetishism, he discovers behind the apparent natural qualities and the apparent social relations of things, the social relations of men, produced historically and both mediated and repressed from consciousness by coercive conditions; and behind the "natural" characteristics of capital an historically produced class relationship.[10] Therefore there is a reciprocally consolidated relationship between historical materialism as a theory of socio-economic development mediated through class struggle, and the criticism of political economy. But if a "modification" of Marx's interpretation of history actually becomes available and if this modified construct is not merely to have the status of a meta-theory of history (unauthoritative in regard to the material contents of the theory), then an inner-theoretical contradiction between the "historical" and the "ideology-critical" theoretical approaches nevertheless has to be established—unless criticism of the objectivistic traces in Marx's philosophy of history, especially his conception of the transition to the classless society, is to mean the total conception of theory. I believe it can be shown that, even to the extent of specific economic analyses, there is an unresolved contradiction between the "modified" historical materialism (that is, that which traces the "dialectics of morality" back to the dialectics of production) and the ideology-critical theoretical approach; and that, in particular, in contrast to this theoretical approach, "modified" historical materialism results in an objectivistic concept of revolution that Marx has at some points explicitly acknowledged as his own.

I shall first of all indicate where this alleged contradiction is to be found. If, on this construction, the human *praxis* which constitutes and transforms society, and with it "production" and the transformation of men's societal consciousness, appear ultimately as derivations and functions of their work in transforming nature, then the dialectical interplay between the world-historical process of formation of consciousness and so-

10. Cf. MA, Vol. 4, pp. 47 ff.

cial institutions on the one hand, and the historical development of productive forces on the other, must be misconceived as a functional relationship. Conditions of production, and ideologies that legitimize domination, then tacitly become second-order productive forces; their history can no longer be reconstructed in practical terms as that of a progressive emancipation from the pressures of naturally effective social repression, instead their sole logic is that of another history: that of the technical conquest of external nature, that is, of the emancipation of men from the natural pressures that restrict them—but emancipation by means of the progressive reification of their "essential powers" in material production. The dissolution of a false social consciousness of a kind that stabilizes domination (for Marx a constitutive aspect of the dissolution of relations of domination in the class struggle) cannot then be conceived as the result of a practical "process of formation"; instead, it must itself reappear as the *product* of social work, that is, as the necessary by-product of socio-economic changes, which for their part were exacted solely by processes of technical innovation. But if the determining relationship between the development of productive forces, the transformation of forms of domination, and transformation of social consciousness, is construed in this way, there are distinct consequences amounting to the establishment of an objectivistic theory of revolution. *Firstly,* the immanent logic of a progressive technological self-objectification of men provides both the goal and the necessary result of human "prehistory," namely, the complete rationalization of the process of social reproduction; *secondly,* the theoretical reconstruction of the prehistorical determining relationship between productive forces, conditions of production, and ideologies, becomes a task for strict experimental science; *thirdly,* there is the result that, in the capitalist process of production, the *subjective* conditions for a revolutionary transition to the classless society must be "produced" at the very same time as the objective conditions; *fourthly,* and finally, the "correct" proletarian

71

consciousness can ultimately be none other than the consciousness of positive science: the freedom of proletarian men is attenuated and blunted to become insight into historical necessity,
and their revolution can merely reduce and alleviate the "birth
pangs" of the new society.

Of course this theoretical relationship is not to be found in
this form anywhere in Marx. But if the more or less evident
"distortions" of Marx's philosophy of history are seen in the
perspective of decisions made in advance on the level of categorization, then they can be presented in terms of that theoretical
relationship as their ideal limit value. This means, however, that
the modification of Marx's construction of history potentially
removes the basis of his critical social theory *qua* ideology-
criticism. For this theory can only be a *critique* of ideology as
a socially necessary illusion, if, as an historically explicative
theory, it simultaneously reveals the contradiction between society as it is, and what it could and must be in terms of its
technical possibilities and of the interpretations of the "good life"
acknowledged within it. This means that critical theory does not
wish to replace an ideological consciousness with a scientific
consciousness, but—of course by means of empirical and historical analyses—to assist the practical reason existing in the
form of ideological consciousness to "call to mind" its distorted
form, and at the same time to get control of its practical-utopian
contents. Ultimately, therefore, critical theory can prove itself
only by initiating a reflective dissolution of false consciousness
resulting in liberating *praxis:* the successful dissolution of false
consciousness as an integrative aspect of emancipatory practice
is the proper touchstone for its truth, because only in the process
of this dissolution and resolution can it exist as the *acknowledged*
truth of false consciousness. The truth of critical social theory
is a *verité à faire;* in the last resort it can demonstrate its truth-
fulness only by successful liberation: hence the hypothetico-
practical status peculiar to the theory.

This hypothetico-practical status (and this is my thesis) is challenged by the basic assumptions of Marx's interpretation of history. In those basic assumptions, technical progress, the abrogation of "dysfunctional" social repression and the dissolution of false consciousness are so indissolubly joined, that the irresistible advance of technical progress, which starts with the capitalist mode of production, has to be interpreted as the irresistible advance towards the commonwealth of freedom. The building of the realm of freedom is therefore shifted back into the same continuum of historical necessity in which, for Marx, the prehistory of the human species had advanced. But on this assumption, the reasonableness of liberating practice can no longer be measured according to the degree to which it has already liberated from the existing coercive context those active individuals who have been enlightened as to their true interest, but only according to the extent to which they act on the basis of insight into the scientifically detectable regularities of the course of history. In this way, there is a potential elimination from the concept of liberating practice of that aspect of a reflective dissolution of false consciousness, which allows the practical realization of critical theory to be distinguished from the practical realization of a strictly experimental scientific theory: Insight into the history and meaning of experienced social bondage and constraint, at which critical theory aims as the precondition of a process of collective emancipation, is indissolubly bound up with the transformation of attitudes, modes of behavior and possibilities of experience; the dissolution of false consciousness mediated through practice *and* self-reflection is therefore at one and the same time transformation of consciousness and transformation of men.[11] Against this, a critical social theory which

11. It is possible to interpret in this sense those statements of Marx's in which he anticipates the necessary transformation of the proletarians as the result of their liberating *praxis*. E.g., in the *Revelations about the Cologne Communist Trial*: "Whereas we say to the workers: You have fifteen, twenty, or even fifty years of civil wars and national wars to

73

is misconceived as a strict experimental scientific theory can no longer anticipate the necessary transformation of men who want to transform society, in the dimension of a self-enlightening *praxis;* instead it must rigorously distinguish between the transformation of consciousness and the transformation of attitudes and modes of behavior: the first becomes knowledge of the economic law of movement of capitalist society, the second must be comprehended as the necessary result of the process of material production.

The basic thesis that I shall now try to establish in greater detail, may be provisionally formulated thus: The union of historical materialism and the criticism of political economy in Marx's social theory is inherently contradictory. In particular, the basic assumptions of Marx's interpretation of history suggest, in contrast to the ideology-critical approach of the theory, an "objectivistic" concept of revolution in a twofold sense: on the one hand, they determine the revolutionary *function* of critical theory as that of a post-ideological, "positive" science, whereas on the other hand they lead to the camouflaging of the distinction between the *inevitable* and the practically necessary transformation of capitalist society, thus allowing the transition to the classless society to appear as the enforced result of the solution of problems proper to the capitalist system.

If this thesis is correct, then two misconceptions of Marx's theory which have certain practical consequences may depend on a theoretical relationship which is more or less latent in this theory itself; I shall call them the "technocratic" and the "evolu-

---

endure, not only in order to change conditions, but in order to change yourselves and to fit yourselves for political rule, you say, on the contrary: 'We must come to power immediately, or else lay ourselves down to rest' " (MA, Vol. 3, i, p. 454). Significantly, in this *political* document Marx stresses the emancipatory function of the class *struggle.* On the other hand, insofar as a modified historical materialism is brought to bear in his theory, precisely this liberating function of the class struggle is neglected in favor of the system-breaking function of objective class *antagonism.*

tionist" misconceptions. According to the first misconception, under certain historic initial conditions socialism would have to be brought about by an exclusive, theoretically trained, revolutionary minority ruling by authoritarian measures; according to the second, it would have to be the enforced result of the development of capitalist society. In fact, as can easily be seen, there is only one misconception: namely, a "mechanistic" misunderstanding of historical materialism, according to which the revolution becomes the mere question of more or less expenses on the bill of history—since the end result of history is already settled. If, however, this error can find support in a theoretical relationship latent in Marx's theory, then a meta-criticism of Marx's critique of political moralism is also requisite; at any rate to the extent that this critique, which struck at the Young Hegelians, early socialists and anarchists with equal severity, understood itself to be precisely the result of the development of socialism from utopia to *science*.

I shall have to preface the following argument with a remark in regard to method. Since in preparing this essay I was concerned to establish a theoretical relationship which often appears in Marx's theory in only a fragmentary form, I have based my argument mainly on those texts in which the relationship in question is explicit. For this reason, *The German Ideology* and some points in the *Outlines of Political Economy* (*Grundrisse . . .*) in particular are stressed to an extent that would be inappropriate in other circumstances. This shift of emphasis is, I think, justified, because in these particular works Marx deduces certain findings from his interpretation of history which make its significance in systematic terms for his conception of revolution stand out very clearly.

In order to show the contradiction *within* Marx's theory quite distinctly, I shall first of all attempt to demonstrate the connection between the young Marx's criticism of ideology and the criticism of political economy.

75

2.

As is known, the young Marx's criticism of ideology, insofar as it is a criticism of the ideology of the constitutional state, is directly indebted to Hegel's historico- and juridico-philosophical examination of the "epoch" of the French Revolution. Hegel had conceived the emancipation of civil society as the realization of "formal" or "abstract" right (law); for him, with the French Revolution "the principle of reason in the shape of the legally guaranteed freedom of all men as individuals had become a reality." [12] But at the same time he had recognized the ambivalence of this positive realization of the universal rights of individual freedom. For Hegel, the liberation of individuals from the "positivity" of historically accidental, substantive ties, the fulfilment of the "development of particularity" in the "form of universality," [13] that actually allowed the emancipated individual of modern times to appear as a "son of civil society," [14] is at one and the same time the loss of substantive morality; civil society is a "system of needs," in which self-subsistent private individuals pursue their selfish ends and satisfy their private needs without reference to any universal interest: the universal aspect of this system—abstract right—is therefore quite decisively opposed to the reasonable universality of a "good life" uniting these private persons. Consequently, civil society is only the realization of an *abstract* freedom the "substance" of which is still "outside it." [15] But that is not all. In Hegel's treatment of civil society it is already apparent that this "apartness" of "abstract" and "substantive" freedom is properly to be understood in an historical sense. For the negativity which he reveals

12. Jürgen Habermas, Postscript to *Hegels politischen Schriften* (Frankfurt, 1966), p. 363.
13. Cf. *Philosophy of Right,* sections 185, 186; see also J. Ritter, *Hegel und die französische Revolution* (Frankfurt am Main, 1965).
14. Cf. *Philosophy of Right,* section 238; Ritter, *op. cit.,* p. 59
15. *Jenenser Realphilosophie,* ed. Hoffmeister.

in civil society is that of its own *law of movement,* by reason of which it must produce a continually self-intensifying antagonism between *classes:* "When civil society operates without impediment [. . .], the amassing of wealth increases [. . .] on the one hand; whereas, on the other hand, there is an intensification of the *subdivision* and *restriction* of labor of a specific kind, and consequently an intensification of the *dependence* and *need* of the class tied to this kind of work." [16] "Through this dialectics," civil society is "driven beyond its own limits"; [17] but, and this is the decisive application of Hegel's notion, it is not driven to an *historical* self-transcendence, that is, a transcendence of the abstract freedom based on private property by the substantial freedom of a fully emancipated society, but to its transcendence in the *state,* which, as a power independent of society, compensates society's lack of substantial morality, so to speak from without. Hegel therefore does not conceive the existing state in terms of the functions of that antagonistic context of coercion which he reveals behind the abstract freedom of civil society, but deduces it from the dialectical logic of a reason which has come to know itself as the "actuality of the ethical idea" [18]: "Through the systematic dialectics which sublates civil society in the state, the dialectics of history is now arrested." [19] The state which checks the egotism of civil society *is,* for Hegel, already the "actuality of concrete freedom"; that is, the reconciliation of the individual with the universal interest, by subjective and objective spirit, the "fusion of the substantial and the particular" by means of which "my obligation to the state becomes at one and the same time the existence of my particular freedom." In the political institutions of the constitutional state, as in the rational sentiments and practice of the citizens, concrete freedom becomes actual as the substance of abstract free-

16. *Philosophy of Right,* section 243.
17. *Ibid.,* section 246.
18. *Ibid.,* section 257.
19. Herbert Marcuse, "Studie über Autorität und Familie," in *Ideen zu einer kritischen Theorie der Gesellschaft* (Frankfurt, 1969), p. 102.

dom: "the absolute morality of an Aristotelian ordering of the good life is reproduced in political power, being only mediated by the system of needs." Marx was to put in question this *systematic* mediation between the system of needs and the substantial freedom of the citizen, by deciphering it simultaneously as the concealment of an *historical* mediation.

Hegel's conception of civil society is a critical recognition of the world-historical significance of the French Revolution and the aspect of truth in its substantiation in natural law. In the natural-law fiction of a natural state of isolated, natural individuals, he of course recognizes the historical character of civil society; its "natural state" is a result of world history. Still wholly along these lines is the following statement of the young Marx: "The *political revolution* dissolves civil life into its component parts [. . .], it views civil society [. . .] as the *basis of its existence,* as a *premiss* that requires no further ground, and hence as its *natural basis.*"[20] Of course Marx has given these propositions a certain critical significance: behind them is his settlement with Hegel's understanding of state law.

This criticism of Hegel by the young Marx is unmistakably tied to a premiss that Hegel had formulated in the *Philosophy of Right:* "The principle of modern states has immense strength and depth inasmuch as it allows the principle of subjectivity to realize itself in the *self-sufficient extreme* of personal particularity, at the same time bringing it back to *substantial unity* and thus maintaining substantial unity in the principle of subjectivity itself."[21] The young Marx recognizes this principle as the more profound principle of the bourgeois revolutions, and at the same time points out, as against Hegel, that it had as yet been acknowledged only in principle but had not been realized in the post-revolutionary state. As yet the fulfillment of the "idealism of the state" is only "the fulfillment of the materialism of civil

20. MA, Vol. 1, p. 478.
21. *Philosophy of Right,* section 260.

society." [22] "The real man is recognized only in the shape of the egotistic individual, the *true* man only in the form of the abstract *citoyen*." [23] As yet all that is *actual* is the *contradiction* between the abstract freedom of isolated private persons and the substantive freedom of associated citizens; the existing state which Hegel saw as the setting-right of this contradiction is in fact only an appendix to a civil society which is, in itself, the practical negation of that substantive freedom. And so Marx now gives a wholly new significance to Hegel's insight that the "man" of the Declarations of the Rights of Man is only the burgher hypostatized as the private individual who is guaranteed scope for the pursuit of his particular material interests: "None of the so-called rights of man goes [. . .] beyond the egotistic man who, as a member of civil society, withdraws into himself, his private interest and his private arbitrary will and is an individual separated from the community. The Rights of Man are far from viewing man as a species-being; instead species-life itself—society—appears as a framework external to the individual, as a restriction of his original independence. The only bond that holds men together is natural necessity, need and private interest, and the preservation of their property and their egotistic persons." [24]

Marx recognizes that the contradiction between formal and substantial freedom is not an antithesis between different aspects of the ethical idea become actual,[25] but that, on the contrary, it must be comprehended as the contradiction between two different historical stages in the history of human emancipation: The *political* emancipation which, with the realization of formal freedom in progressive civil societies has simultaneously made these societies the location of a naked *"bellum omnium contra*

22. MA, Vol. 1, p. 477.
23. *Op. cit.*, p. 478.
24. MA, Vol. 1, p. 474.
25. Cf. *Philosophy of Right*, section 257.

omnes" (war of all against all),[26] is still to be followed by *human* emancipation as the realization of the substantive freedom of all men.[27] In this way Marx perceives the philosophical justification of the existing state to be a piece of "furtive theology"; just as the criticism of religion discovered in "religious misery" not only the "expression of real misery" but *"protest against real misery,"* [28] the criticism of right (law) and politics will find in the ideological justification of actual society the weapons for the struggle against this society.

In this sense Marx developed, in a letter to Arnold Ruge of September 1843, a strategy of radical enlightenment the principles of which are those of an immanent criticism: Criticism must make manifest as a practical task the utopian contents developed in the bourgeois revolutions and in their ideological self-representations, in contrast to the irrationality of existing social conditions: "Reason has always existed, but not always in a rational form. Hence the critic can begin with any form of theoretical and practical consciousness and develop the true actuality from the forms *peculiar to* existing reality as that which it ought to be and its ultimate goal. As far as actual life is concerned, it is precisely the *political state* in all its *modern* forms that contains the demands of reason, even where that state is not yet consciously aware of socialist demands. And it does not stop at that. Everywhere the political state represents reason as realized. But at the same time it falls into the contradiction between its ideal nature and its actual presuppositions. Therefore social truth can be developed everywhere from this conflict of the political state with itself." [29] This would also seem to satisfy Hegel's criticism of the abstract "ought-to-be." For the critic does not present the world dogmatically with entirely new principles, but "develops new principles for the world from the

26. MA, Vol. 1, p. 463.
27. *Op. cit.,* p. 456.
28. Cf. *op. cit.,* p. 488.
29. *Op. cit.,* p. 448.

principles of the world." [30] Then it will be evident, Marx believes, "that the world has long possessed the dream of something of which it need only become conscious in order to possess it in actuality." [31]

To what extent did this ideology-critical approach of the young Marx, which is still very close to Hegel's position in the Frankfurt years,[32] enter into his later theory? There was a decisive step still to be taken: the "existing contradiction" posited by Marx had to be decoded as an actual antagonism of social interests, before it could become the starting point for an historical liberating movement. Otherwise the playing-off of idea against reality, of the substantive freedom of the *citoyen* against the merely formal freedom of egotistic private persons, would—despite everything—have been *moral* criticism, and the position of the later Hegel more consequential. In other words: Marx's hypothesized *historical* contradiction between the abstract freedom of civil society and the concrete freedom of a truly emancipated society would have to be proven to be at the same time an irreconcilable and potentially system-breaking antagonism in the foundations of civil society itself. To do this it was not enough to identify the proletariat as a class with "radical chains" whose total alienation comprised interest in a "radical revolution"; instead, the existence of this class, "which owns nothing but its ability to work," had to be shown to be at one and the same time "a necessary prerequisite of capital" [33] as well as the factor determining the abolition of capital.

With a critique of political economy based on the theory of labor value, Marx completes this step beyond the mere criticism

30. *Op. cit.*, p. 449.
31. *Op. cit.*, p. 450.
32. Cf. Jürgen Habermas, Postscrift to *Hegels politischen Schriften*, pp. 354 ff.
33. Already in "Wage Labor and Capital," MA, Vol. 6, p. 773.

of the ideology of the bourgeois constitutional state. But the criticism of political economy is also the execution of this criticism of ideology in a more sequacious form. Since the theory of labor value provides the key to the problems unsolved by classical political economy, it reveals the true nature of an abstract freedom dependent on private ownership, and the ideological nature of its justifications. The actual "substance" of the abstract freedom of civil society is now recognizable as class antagonism, the exploitation of wage labor by capital, the "substantive" bondage of the proletariat. This continually growing proletariat is identifiable as the historical subject for which the *practical* necessity of an abrogation of private ownership of the means of production becomes a necessity *of existence.*

Even with this materialistic application, the criticism of ideology (and this is a provisional answer to the question posed above) is still bound up with an idea of freedom which it must presuppose as the rational core, the utopian content, of the systems of legitimation that it criticizes, in order to be *criticism* at all. Hence not this distinguishes it from the ideology criticism of the young Marx, but its attachment now to an exhibition of the historical tendencies which in a specific sense make the "realization of philosophy" an objective possibility. The rise of the proletariat is only one side of the question. The other side, namely, the inherently progressive significance of the capitalist mode of production in regard to the realization of the "concrete" freedom of an emancipated society, had already been emphasized by Marx in the *Communist Manifesto.* Accordingly, the bourgeoisie is the revolutionary class *par excellence;* its emancipation, that is, the carrying-through of the capitalist mode of production, first of all provides the material and spiritual prerequisites of a universal human emancipation. For the first time in history the continuous revolutionizing of production has become the condition of existence of a ruling class. This means: *firstly,* that the technical prerequisites have been provided for an abolition of exploitation of men by men, that is, for a uni-

LATENT POSITIVISM OF MARX'S PHILOSOPHY OF HISTORY

versal human emancipation in the sense of the building of a classless society; *secondly,* that as a result of the expansionist tendencies of capital, and the consequent universal spread of the capitalist mode of production, the prerequisites have been produced for a universal human emancipation in the sense of *world* revolution; *thirdly,* that with the political centralization exacted by the centralizing tendencies of capital, and with the combination of workers made possible by technical, economic and political changes, the *political* requisites have been provided for the planning and execution of a socialist revolution; and it also means, *fourthly,* that with the dissolution of all traditional forms of life exacted by the revolutionizing of production, with the permanent alteration of all determining factors of social life, the *spiritual* (mental) prerequisites have been provided for a revolution carried out in full consciousness. The evident resolution of "personal worth" into "exchange value," and the realization of "all that is solid melts into air, all that is holy is profaned," simultaneously abolish all ideologies that legitimize domination: "Man is at last compelled to face with sober senses, his real conditions of life, and his relations with his kind." [34]

Of course the fact of a "disillusionment" of the proletarian masses that is bound up with the experience of radical alienation does not imply that a correct concept of possible social freedom, associated as an "idea" with the suppressed interest, must become material force. The "spontaneously" arising disillusionment of men on the contrary provides merely the prerequisites of a process of enlightenment that succeeds only on resulting in a class war conducted consciously, that is, from a perception of the objective conditions and of practical necessity. The medium of this enlightenment is theory, whose destruction of ideology through the analysis of the context of social coercion must also be the disclosure of a concept of possible social free-

34. Marx, *Frühschriften,* ed. Landshut (Stuttgart, 1953), p. 529.

dom, which, as the "real" utopian content of false social consciousness, it can obtain only in the course of this criticism. This means, however, that—by means of the analysis of society —theory must at the same time reconstruct the repressed interest of individuals as rational interest: the rational can only become the object of interest, when the interest becomes an interest enlightened as to its own rationality, and when the satisfaction of the repressed interest is conceived as truly rational. But if the idea of social freedom, whose historically concrete forms became the guideline of criticism, can become a *rational* concept of *possible* social freedom only by means of the critical analysis of society, then this means, too, that only the historico-materialistic decyphering of the philosophy of the spirit can give the intention to realize philosophy a rational significance. In this sense, the abovementioned provisional answer to the question of the connection between the ideology-critical approach of the young Marx and his historically oriented social theory needs modification.

We had already seen that the meaning of "ideology criticism" in Marx's economic writings remained the same as in the early Marx, insofar as the destruction of ideology in the criticism of political economy can still be read in the practical intention to "realize philosophy." However, a more thorough analysis shows that talk of the realization of philosophy can be taken in a purely metaphorical sense in the early Marx as well. When Marx criticizes Hegel's philosophy as being not self-consciousness of the actual but the false consciousness of what is to be realized, that alone decides that this philosophy is just as little able to answer the question of *what* ought to be realized in practice, as the question of what is false in this philosophy itself. In other words: philosophy does not become rational by removing its presupposition that the rational is already actual, as if that presupposition were an avoidable hypothesis; on the contrary, criticism of this presupposition concerns Hegelian philosophy as a whole, so that the rational thing that is to be realized also has

84

to be released from its "irrational" philosophical covering. This simple consideration already shows that there is a prejudgment in the young Marx's ideology criticism: in playing off the utopian against the ideological contents of philosophy and of the dominant social consciousness, it relies on reference to a social and historical theory which can really enlighten the existing consciousness as to its ideological contents and thereby recall to it the real meaning of its utopian contents, only by reconstructing society and its ideological contents as an historically developed society and consciousness. Precisely because the Hegel-criticism of the young Marx is criticism with a *practical purpose,* its ideology-critical approach must lead it to a materialistic "reversal" of Hegel's philosophy of spirit; only with this reversal is the historico-philosophical consciousness so to speak put into a "rational form"; [35] only then does the criticism of the ideology of bourgeois society acquire a proficient basis. Together with the criticism of political economy, historical materialism provides the reconstruction of that crisis-laden context of coercion and guilt which signifies the history of the rise of humanity, the context whose access to consciousness alone can turn utopian thought pressing towards reality into thought towards which reality itself thrusts.

The foregoing is a summary account of the systematic value of historical materialism, the elements of which Marx developed for the first time in the *Economic and Philosophical Manuscripts,* significantly enough, in conjunction with a first critique of political economy. By conceiving history as the process of self-creation of the human species through social labor, he begins to evolve the historico-philosophical equipment which he was to use in completing the demythologization of Hegel's interpretation of history—the inadequacy of which we have already seen from the *Introduction to a Critique of Hegel's Philosophy of Right.* Only historical materialism, by displaying the "mechanisms" of human evolution and of historical development,

35. Cf. MA, Vol. 1, p. 448.

provides the key for a materialistic interpretation of the historico-philosophical trope: "alienation—transcendence of alienation." Historical materialism provides (or should provide) the categories in which the revolutionary transition can be theoretically anticipated as a practical process, and therefore the basis for the conception of revolutionary theory as a theory of revolution.

3.

An analysis of the relationship between his criticism of Hegel's constitutional law and his criticism of political economy shows clearly that Marx's theory operates by means of a system of reference in which the criticism of "alienated politics" must become the criticism of "alienated labor," just as the criticism of alienated labor must become the criticism of alienated politics. The "transcendence of the alienation" of man from the objectifications of his own "essential powers" therefore always has a twofold meaning for Marx: abrogation of alienated work and humanization of alienated *praxis,* so that both aspects constitute one another reciprocally. That men "appropriate" to themselves the product of their alienated labor, also means that they transform the institutions of their social life, which have become an alien force dominating them, into the institutions of freely associated citizens. Only on this basis can they eventually recognize themselves in their self-objectifications and therefore in one another. The application of this idea in the writings of the young Marx is the beginning of an historico-materialistic explication of the idea of a reciprocal liberation of man in the citizen, and of the citizen in man, which Marx freed from Hegel's affirmative historico-philosophical interpretation of the Prussian state as the utopian content of that interpretation, thus making it the guiding principle of the criticism of ideology. As we saw, Marx recognized in this idea the reason of the bourgeois age, reason preparing itself in the proletariat for its expression

86

in practice. This idea was, in fact, already programmatically and practically anticipated in the major revolutions of the eighteenth century. Hannah Arendt has again shown this to be true of the self-conception of the revolutionary leaders in the discussions about the constitution and in the "soviet-republican" approaches of both revolutions.[36] Only because Marx could rely on a revolutionary tradition, in which the intentions of achieving the freedom of the individual and personal happiness were already more or less clearly bound up with the idea of a public political arena constituted by citizens able to communicate with one another without coercion, and with the ideas of *public* freedom and *public* happiness, was the young Marx's critique of Hegel able to become a criticism of the ideology of the bourgeois constitutional state of the advanced Western type. Marx was able fundamentally to radicalize Hegel's criticism of a civil society "given up to itself" only because the movements of civil emancipation themselves had afforded a substantive concept of social freedom whose recognition already implies the judgment of the post-revolutionary society.

If we accept that Marx's reconstruction of history as a history of class struggles provided, together with the critique of political economy, a suitable materialistic reformulation of the concept of political freedom already anticipated in revolutionary tradition, we must ask what this theory has to say about the revolutionary process to which it looks forward. The question cannot be answered in full here; nevertheless, a clear idea of the bases of possible answers is requisite.

Marx conceives his critical theory as part of a critical *praxis,* which, as the class struggle of the proletariat, has already as-

36. Cf. Hannah Arendt, *Über die Revolution* (Munich, 1963), Chapters 4 to 5. The fact that otherwise Hannah Arendt virtually turns upside down the connection between the social and political liberation movements of modern times is quite another matter. Cf., on this point, Jürgen Habermas, "Die Geschichte von den zwei Revolutionen," in *Merkur,* 1966, 5.

sumed an historical form. In a certain sense, the theory can be comprehended as the "self-consciousness" of this class struggle: it is the consciousness of the social situation and of the historic task of the proletariat. The social situation of the proletariat and the existence of the theory itself offer the possibility that the proletariat, as the first and last class in history, will conduct a class war *in consciousness* of its determining factors, possibilities and goals. But what are the consequences in regard to the chances of success of the revolutionary struggle? One is that the abolition of capitalist private ownership will succeed as the *transition to the classless society,* if a proletariat that is not only ready for the struggle, but also enlightened, sees and seizes its chance in the final crisis of the capitalist system predicted by theory. However, the "enlightenment" of the proletariat can be anticipated only as a protracted process of practical emancipation, which must already begin *within* the capitalist system, and in which, with the dissolution of false consciousness, the attitudes, modes of behavior and abilities of men will also change. Therefore the connection between enlightenment, practical emancipation, and liberating practice, implies that in the forms of organization and in the principles of the revolutionary movement, certain elements of future social freedom must already be realized, if the revolution is to signify the realization of this social freedom.

Consequently, an essential decision about the fate of the revolution is already comprised in the "process of education" of the revolutionary class; in the course of that education it is ultimately decided whether, in a revolutionary crisis, enlightened individuals acting in solidarity will be able to apply the *"Constitutio Libertatis"* that was merely promised by the bourgeois revolutions.

Marx often acknowledges this "openness" of the revolutionary process. Thus he stresses the necessity of protracted revolutionary processes of instruction only by means of which the proletariat will be able to acquire the maturity requisite for the assumption of political power;[37] at one point he speaks of the "vague immensity" of the revolutionary project, whose goals could be concretized and brought closer to realization only by means of a continuous process of critical auto-correction, both of theory and of the revolutionary movement itself. However, he would seem, by and large, to have considered that the ultimate success of the revolution was inevitable. But here a prejudgment is evident that has a dual basis in Marx's interpretation of history: this interpretation neither allows the revolutionary process to be seriously comprehended as a process of enlightenment on the success of which the success of the revolution is ultimately dependent, nor does it permit an appropriate materialistic explication and criticism of the bourgeois concept of political freedom from which *practical* norms for revolutionary can be deduced. The two are closely connected: processes of collective enlightenment can be anticipated only on the premiss of a normative concept of autonomy and "undistorted" communication. Understood as a process of enlightenment, the revolutionary process is subject to norms the explication of which is at one and the same time an explication of the political freedom to be realized, and the fulfillment of which, moreover, no historic destiny can guarantee.

I shall now attempt to show how Marx's approach to the interpretation of history involves a repudiation of these implications of his approach to the criticism of ideology.

4.

I shall begin with a description of the concept of ideology that Marx developed in connection with his exposition of historical materialism. This concept of ideology is peculiarly far behind the ideology-critical approach of his theory; he no longer allows it to comprehend the dissolution of false consciousness as a process of emancipation mediated through communicative *praxis*

37. Cf., e.g., MA, Vol. 3, i, p. 454.

and reflection; the premisses of his interpretation of history on the contrary require Marx to conceive the development of social consciousness as a direct function of the development of the material production process. Thereby, however, he tacitly makes the historic process itself once again the guarantor of the future *correct* consciousness of the revolutionary masses, admittedly this time under materialistic presuppositions. In *The German Ideology* it is possible to trace the course of this transformation of the ideology-critical approach into the reference-system of a modified historical materialism.

Here Marx no longer speaks of ideological formations of consciousness in the sense of a reason existing only in its in-authentic form as a utopian consciousness *inverted* for the justi-fication of domination. Ideology is rather merely the actuality of a form of class domination apprehended in thought. Ideol-ogies are no longer "ideas of domination" in the sense that in them the rational appears inverted in the interests of domina-tion, but in the "instrumental" sense of a superstructure that maintains domination.[38]

"The dominant ideas are no more than the ideal expression of the dominant material relations, the dominant material rela-tions apprehended as ideas; hence the relations which make one class the dominant class, hence the ideas of its domination. The individuals who go to make up the dominant class possess con-sciousness, among other things, and therefore think; therefore, insofar as they rule as a class and determine the entire extent of an historical epoch, it is self-evident that they do this in their entire range, that is, among other things, they dominate as think-ers, as producers of ideas who control the production and dis-tribution of the ideas of their own times . . ."[39] As "ideas of

38. Cf. Karl Marx and Friedrich Engels, *Werke,* Vol. 3 (Berlin, 1962), p. 46. (This edition of the Works is referred to thereafter as *MEW.*)
39. MEW, p. 46.

domination," ideologies are the illusions of a ruling class which help to ensure domination, and at the same time the illusions of the dominated; [40] a limited truth is to be attributed to them only insofar as the actual practice of men is reflected in them (in this sense they are the "conscious existence" of men), but not because an interest in reason, even in an inverted form, expresses itself in them.

This is only apparently contradicted when Marx says that "every new class [. . .] is forced to represent its interest as the common interest of all members of society, that is, expressed in an ideal form: it has to give its ideas the form of universality and to represent them as the only rational, universally valid ideas." [41] For Marx no longer views reason in general as one which, even in its inverted forms, is already "on the way to itself"; on the contrary, the illusion of rationality is, so to speak, a formal desideratum which every inauthentic form of social consciousness must satisfy in order to be a *dominant* consciousness. Marx takes his criticism of the idealism of *"Geistesgeschichte"* (the history of pure thought) to the point where the tracks of *its* own history are effaced from objective spirit (mind), and that history is replaced by the autonomous history of material production. The history of consciousness becomes the reflex of actual history: "The starting point is real, active men; the development of the ideological reflexes and echoes of their actual process of life is represented on the basis of that process. The phantastic images in the brains of men are also necessary sublimates of their material process of life, which is empirically verifiable and attached to material premises. Morality, religion, metaphysics and the rest of ideology and their corresponding forms of consciousness therefore no longer keep the illusion of autonomy. They have no history, and no development; for men, developing their material production and their material inter-

40. Cf. *op. cit.*, p. 47.
41. *Op. cit.*, p. 47.

course, transform their thinking and the products of their thinking as they transform this reality." [42]

False consciousness now becomes a function of relations of dominance, no longer merely in its falsity, but in all its contents; this functionalization of forms of social consciousness in regard to forms of domination is of course only possible to this radical degree because the history of forms of domination is again reduced to another history—that of material production itself.

At this point the substantial consequences of the modification of the categorical framework are clear so far as the interpretation of history is concerned. Marx has to deduce the various forms of domination directly from various forms of productive labor, because the sole logic of history which can still be permitted in a materialistic reference-system which reduces the dialectics of morality to that of production is the logic of the history of the progressive technological self-objectification of men. According to this logic, the forms of social intercourse can be apprehended, so to speak, only as secondary productive forces, whose function is to make possible the application and development of the primary productive forces: "These different conditions, which first of all appear as conditions of self-activity, but later as its fetters, form in the entire development of history a connected series of forms of intercourse, the connection of which consists in [!] the fact that an earlier form of intercourse which has become a fetter is replaced by a new one, corresponding to the more developed forces of production and therefore to the more advanced form of self-activity of individuals: this new form of intercourse in its turn becomes a fetter and is then replaced by another. As these conditions correspond at every stage to the simultaneous development of productive forces, their history is simultaneously the history of the self-developing productive forces taken over by each new generation, and is

42. *Op. cit.*, pp. 26 ff.

therefore the history of development of the forces of individuals themselves." [43]

Of course Marx emphasizes the fact (and the passage cited above allows a corresponding interpretation) that the various aspects of a social life-context—productive forces, forms of intercourse, ideologies—have to be observed "in their totality," "and therefore the interplay of these aspects too." [44] But he can only justify this kind of "totalizing" approach on the basis of his systematic approach if he includes in the sphere of material production itself, so to speak as mere control mechanisms, aspects of the social life-context which are primarily distinct from material production; the "interplay" between productive forces and forms of intercourse then consists in, say, this: not only that specific productive forces "produce" or "condition" specific forms of intercourse, but that, on the other hand, specific forms of intercourse first make possible and give rise to a development of existing productive forces. In precisely this way, then, every "corresponding" form of intercourse (as the "mode of cooperation" of men in society itself) is—a "productive force." [45] The categorical framework of Marx's interpretation of history essentially allows the "totality" of an historico-social life-context to be apprehended only as that of a self-regulated dynamic system, which possesses, as it were, only one type of freedom of historical development: that of technical innovation. Innovations in the sub-system of production give rise to displacements of equilibrium, which have then to be removed by adaptation of the sub-system of institutions to that of production. This adaptation, however, is to be comprehended as the "technically," straightforwardly defined solution of a systematic problem.

This re-interpretation of historical materialism does not, of course, correspond to the materialistic conception of history as

43. *Op. cit.*, p. 72.
44. *Op. cit.*, p. 38.
45. *Op. cit.*, p. 30.

a history of class struggles. However, this is a matter of the incompatibility of two conceptions which Marx himself tries in vain to cover up, as can be seen from his concept of a "contradiction" between productive forces and conditions of production.

"All collisions in history," says *The German Ideology*,[46] "[. . .] originate, in our view, in the contradiction between the productive forces and the form of intercourse." "This contradiction [. . .] had on every occasion to break out in a revolution, assuming at the same time various subsidiary forms: comprehensive collisions, collisions of different classes, contradiction of consciousness, battle of ideas, and so on, class warfare, and so on." Marx distinguishes a basic form of social contradiction from its "subsidiary forms"; the mistake of written history in the past was that in any particular case it made one of these subsidiary forms the basis of social upheavals and historical development in general. "From a restricted viewpoint one can isolate one of these subsidiary forms and see it as the basis of these revolutions—this is all the easier because the very individuals who started the revolutions had illusions about their own activity according to the extent of their education and the stage of historical development."

In what sense can it be said now that a "collision" between classes is the "subsidiary form" of a contradiction between productive forces and forms of intercourse? Does it mean that this contradiction can be detected independently of the social conflicts in which it manifests itself, that is, as the dysfunctionality of a form of domination in regard, say, to the systematic goal of a development of the productive forces? Or does it mean only that the calling-in-question of a dominant order, manifest in class conflict, would only be possible and could only be resolved through the development of the productive forces? In one case, class conflict would be the necessary *consequence* of

46. *Op. cit.*, p. 73.

an "objective" contradiction; in the other case, it would constitute it only *as* contradiction in the general sense. The incompatibility of these two possible interpretations, which are still
left open here, is the incompatibility of two different versions
of historical materialism made plain in the well-known formulations of the *Preface to a Contribution to the Critique of Political
Economy:* "In the social production of their life, men enter into
certain necessary relations that are independent of their will,
relations of production which correspond to a certain stage of
development of their material productive forces. [. . .] At a
certain stage of their development, the material productive forces
of society come into conflict with the existing relations of production, or—what is only a legal expression for those same
relations—with the property relations within which they have
acted until now. These relations turn from forms of development of productive forces into their fetters. Then an epoch of
social revolution commences. With the transformation of the
economic basis, the whole immense superstructure is more slowly
or more speedily transformed. When considering such trans-
formations, one must always make a distinction between the
material transformation of the economic conditions of production, which can be determined with natural scientific exactitude,
and the legal, political, religious, artistic or philosophical, or,
in short, the ideological forms in which men become conscious
of this conflict and fight it out. Just as one does not judge an
individual by what he thinks of himself, so such an epoch of
transformation cannot be judged by its consciousness; instead,
this consciousness must be explained on the basis of the contradictions of material life, of the existing conflict between the
social productive forces and relations of production." [47]
    Here Marx states clearly that social revolutions solve social
systematic problems which are reflected in men's consciousness
but which are defined—independently of the interpretations of

47. MA, Vol. 6, pp. 838 ff.

the individuals concerned—as conflicts "of material life"; hence there are necessary solutions (independent of human volition) to such systematic problems in the shape of a transition to the next, higher mode of production, which in each particular case guarantees the further reproduction of society and the possibility of further development of the productive forces. Each stage of development of the productive forces allows, so to speak, only *one* definite institutionalization of the social reproduction process; hence the class struggle is necessary in order to carry out these institutionalizations, but it is at the same time merely the vehicle of an historical progress which advances to completion behind the backs of the warring classes, and whose unique logic is that of a progressive conquest of external nature by means of a species subject only apparently split into classes.

That is the first of the alternative possible interpretations proposed above; it appears irreconcilable with Marx's intentions. But the second possible interpretation, which takes into account the ideology-critical approach of the theory, is for its part equally incompatible with the text just cited. It would mean that a "conflict" between the productive forces and forms of intercourse was always to be understood *also* as the protest of repressed individuals against forms of domination whose legitimations had become questionable, and against the burdens and deprivations demanded by such forms of dominations and experienced as capricious and unjust. It would be a conflict between the *possibility* of a "good life" anticipated by these very individuals (admittedly on the basis of a definite stage of development of productive forces), and the social constraint that they experience in reality; between the demands of an inherited (that is, traditional) form of domination and the realizable demands of repressed classes. The social conflicts would be those of *material life,* because they would be grounded in the discrepancy between the possible fulfillment and the actual suppression of real needs; but they would be *conflicts* only because,

96

through the interpretation and legitimation of their needs, social groups would put themselves in conflict with the traditional interpretations and legitimations of existing relations of domination. This would mean, however, that the forms in which men became conscious of their social conflicts, and in which they fought them out, would be not only an epiphenomenon of "objective" conflicts between productive forces and conditions of production, but their constitutive aspect (*Moment*). The ideology-critical tracing back of these forms as forms of a distorted ethical context of relations could not be carried out solely by recourse to the "transformation[s] of the economic conditions of production, which can be determined with natural scientific exactitude"; on the contrary, it would first of all require recourse to an immanently critical dissolution of their false consciousness.

Marx's formulations feature an ambiguity which is difficult to resolve, inasmuch as they can be interpreted according to differing theoretical approaches. Hence the program of a transition from ideology to science, already indicated in the confrontation of an ideological consciousness requiring enlightenment with an explicative theory on the basis of facts "which can be determined with natural scientific exactitude," as described by Marx in *The German Ideology,* also appears ambivalent. Nevertheless it is to be interpreted here in the perspective of our ideal-typical re-interpretation of a modified historical materialism.

The fact that Marx believes that the time has come for a transition from the "ideological" to the "scientific" method of observation of social reality is linked with his assumption that the capitalist process of production itself abolishes the traditional legitimations of domination, insofar as uprooted and pauperized men themselves are at last forced to "contemplate their mutual relations with sober eyes." For Marx, "sober" means empirico-scientific, without any premises other than those which are "open to confirmation in a purely empirical fashion." [48] With the confrontation of ideology and science he

97

returns to a certain extent from the shadowland of idealistic dialectics to the firm ground of the empiricist-materialistic tradition, whose enthusiasm for "immediacy," especially that of Feuerbach's philosophy with its "starting point in the positive, the sensuously definite," [49] has left definite traces in this opposition. Nevertheless the influence of Feuerbach, whom Marx had already criticized in *The German Ideology* in regard to a return to insights of idealistic philosophy, has affected only the externals of Marx's thought; its essential content is already determined by the criticism of Feuerbach's materialism and of the whole materialistic tradition. The decisive indication of this is to be found in the second of the *Theses on Feuerbach:* "The question whether human thinking can arrive at objective truth is not a theoretical but a *practical* question. Man has to prove the truth, that is, the reality and power, the 'this-sidedness' of his thinking, in practice." [50] However, for Marx the paradigm for a theoretical truth that proves itself in practice (that is, "through the mediation of industry") was that of natural science.[51] This shows clearly the sole standpoint from which Marx was able to carry out a purely functional conjunction of ideologies and forms of domination: the standpoint *of* empirical science—the only one to have shown its practical truth in contrast to the destruction of ideological illusion. It is now evident how closely interwoven are Marx's interpretation of history, his modification of the concept of ideology and his pragmatic concept of theory, and how, from this reciprocal dependence of various aspects of his theory, the misconception that the end of ideology was identical with the transition from ideology to "positive science" could arise. "Where speculation ceases, there in real life, real, positive science begins—the representation of

48. *Op. cit.,* p. 20.
49. Cf. *Economic and Philosophical Manuscripts,* MA, Vol. 1, p. 639, pp. 603 ff.
50. MEW, Vol. 3, p. 5.
51. Cf. *Economic and Philosophical Manuscripts,* p. 603.

the practical activity, of the practical process of human development." [52]

Originally, Marx viewed ideology as reason in its non-rational form; as conscious being it was *praxis* apprehended in thought, illusion ensuring domination and uncomprehended utopia simultaneously. Revolutionary *praxis* could therefore start from an already actually existent and recognized (that is, embodied in traditions and institutions) outline of meaning. But when Marx rejects all rationally anticipatory aspects of ideology, he discredits at one and the same time the intention to transcend philosophy by its realization. Later, in the *Grundrisse,* he stated this clearly; there he speaks of the "error of those socialists, especially the French, who would interpret socialism as the realization of ideas of civil society that were not discovered by the French Revolution, but brought into circulation in the course of history," and then explains unequivocally: "What distinguishes these socialists from bourgeois apologists is on the one hand their feeling for the contradictions of the system, and on the other the utopianism which consists in not grasping the necessary difference between the real and the ideal forms of civil society, and therefore in undertaking the superfluous task of trying to actualize all over again what is the ideal expression, the transfigured and reflected image thrown off by reality as such itself." [53]

This radicalization of the criticism of ideology would be consistent in the sense of a criticism of a utopian sentiment of the revolutionary movement that was in itself still ideological; [54] however, it signifies more than this, namely, that a critical theory

52. MEW, Vol. 3, p. 27.
53. *Grundrisse* . . . (Berlin, 1953), p. 916.
54. Cf. K. Kosik, *Dialektik des Konkreten* (Frankfurt, 1967), pp. 165 ff.

of the necessity, meaning and goal of revolution transformed by the *practical* reform of ideology (its dissolution) into a science without presuppositions (that is, obeying no premiss but prerequisite social reality) [55] can and must operate only on the basis of the facts, which are "empirically ascertainable." Just as all the information of consciousness to date was "conditioned" by a specific stage of development of the productive forces and of the forms of intercourse "produced" by that stage of development, so in its lack of presuppositions, this revolutionary science is conditioned by the development of the capitalist mode of production; equally, this lack of premisses is its truth: it enables the proletarians (who have become just as devoid of "presuppositions") willingly and consciously to fulfill the scientifically detected law of their history. But when critical theory becomes science in this sense, then, in the historical necessity which is for the first time objectifiable, which means to be seized consciously, there is also to be found the guarantee of future freedom: now, of course, a freedom whose concrete determinations are no longer to be discerned critically by recourse to traditions, but to be obtained directly from the scientific reconstruction of history. But the historical necessity by means of which the transition to the classless society has to occur, must exist in the same dimension of functionally necessary alterations to the system in which human "prehistory" had occurred; with one difference: that this necessity has become ascertainable to the extent that class domination, and with it ideology, have become "dysfunctional" once and for all.

This kind of schematic reinterpretation of Marx's ideas is requisite in order to make clear the objectivism of his theory of revolution in its specifically materialistic phase. This objectivism is expressed in the peculiar way in which, for Marx, the "material conditions" for the transition to the classless society are at the same time *sufficient* conditions: "The bourgeois conditions of production comprise the last antagonistic form of the social

55. Cf. MEW, Vol. 3, p. 27.

production process, [. . .] but the productive forces developing in the womb of civil society at the same time provide the material conditions for the dissolution of this antagonism. Consequently, [!] the prehistory of human society closes with this social formation." [56] Just as, in regard to the social-system problems arising in history hitherto, there was always only one so to speak technically and unambiguously prescribed solution (transition to the next, higher mode of production), whose realization was of course possible only by means of the struggle of the repressed against the ruling class, by means of an apparently self-evolving dialectics of morality, so in regard to the system problems arising with the capitalist mode of production there is only *one* solution: transition to the classless society. Even in this case, class struggle is a necessary motor of social progress, but in such a way that the direction, goal and results of this struggle can be determined unequivocally in advance. *Therefore* it is not a question of "what this or that proletarian or even the entire proletariat may happen to *imagine* on a particular occasion. It is a question of *what it is,* and of what, in accordance with this *being,* it is forced to do historically." [57] And: "Communism for us is not a *state of things* that ought to be made to exist, an *ideal* by which reality has to orient itself. We call communism the *real* movement which transcends the existing state of things. The determining factors of this movement are obtained from the premiss existing now."

It would be inappropriate to remove such uncompromising statements entirely from the context of the criticism of ideology in which, in Marx, they have—initially—a definite *polemical* significance. On the other hand, the foregoing analysis reveals clearly the violent twist of construction needed to give such statements, even out of their particular polemical context, a specific theoretical emphasis that would make them pronouncements about an objectifiable historical necessity. However,

56. MA, Vol. 6, p. 840.
57. MA, Vol. 1, p. 705.

should the objective historical movement which Marx detected really lead to the classless society by way of the "dissolution" of private property and the dissolution of religious and political ideologies, Marx would, so to speak, still have to reveal the historical mechanism that *would have* ultimately to transform the constrained wage laborers—beyond all risks, errors and failures of the revolutionary class-struggle—into the "fully developed individuals" of post-revolutionary society.

In other words: If Marx wanted to adhere to the idea that the "goal" and "action" of the proletariat were "irrevocably marked out" in its own life situation, then, just as much as for the past world-historical "transitions," for the expected transition to the classless society he would have to demythologize the "necessity" of a dialectical logic of history understood in an idealistic sense, into the "necessity" of an historical compulsion taking effect in conditions of historical contingency; he would have to show that the development of the capitalist mode of production and the now inevitable solution of the problems of the capitalist system necessarily implied the transition to the realm of freedom. In fact Marx does attempt, on occasion, materialistically to establish the "transcendence of alienation" as the existentially necessary result of alienation carried to extremes, and at the same time as the sole solution of a problem of social survival.

"Things have now come so far," says, for example, *The German Ideology,* "that individuals have to appropriate the existing totality of productive forces, not only in order to attain to their own self-activity, but above all to safeguard their very existence." [58] In his development of this passage, Marx makes clear that he not only views the abolition of private property as a question of the very existence of the proletariat, and therefore ultimately of society, but that he considers that this abolition of private property will be possible only as a specific mode of

58. MEW, Vol. 3, p. 67.

appropriation of the forces of production by "united individuals." This appropriation can no longer be "restricted," as "all earlier revolutionary appropriations" necessarily were. For the appropriation of "productive forces which have been developed into a totality and which exist only within a universal intercourse" must itself necessarily possess a "universal character," and from two aspects. *Firstly,* it must be equivalent to the "development of a totality of abilities in the individuals themselves"; under the compulsion of technical and economic development itself, this appropriation abolishes the subordination of individuals to the division of labor and to the instruments of production made by them. *Secondly,* the universal character of appropriation is "conditioned by the way in which it has to be carried out" (that is, can only be carried out): "It can be carried out only through a union, which by reason of the nature of the proletariat itself can only be a universal one, and through a revolution in which on the one hand the power of the mode of production and intercourse and of social organization hitherto is overthrown, and on the other hand the universal nature of the proletariat, and the energy it requires to effect the revolution are developed; and in which the proletariat abolishes everything that it still retains from its previous societal position." [59]

The last half of the sentence, in which Marx indicates what the revolution must necessarily accomplish in the proletariat, makes clear the "excess" of practical compared to historical existential necessity in the conception of the proletarian revolution. For the rest, however, Marx's argument is designed precisely to remove this distinction. The necessary universality of appropriation in the twofold sense of a universal union of individuals and the universal unfolding of their capacities he deduces solely from the nature of the existing productive forces and forms of intercourse, from the character of the proletariat and from necessary requirements of revolutionary strategy. But this only serves to *conceal* the fact that the goal of the revolution

59. *Op. cit.,* p. 68.

103

mediated through theory *qua criticism* is not also its scientifically objectifiable and, so to speak, systematically requisite result. For, in actuality, apparently identical determinations now conceal radically different contents; this becomes evident when Marx formulates the *goal* of the revolution: "Only at this stage does self-activity coincide with material life, which corresponds to the development of individuals into full individuals and the throwing-off of all natural restriction; then also the transformation of labor into self-activity corresponds to the transformation of hitherto restricted intercourse into the intercourse of individuals as such." [60]

This point becomes self-evident on comparing the foregoing passage with an analogous passage in *Capital,* in which the "modified meaning" of the historico-philosophical schema "alienation—transcendence of alienation" (which became inevitable in the reference system of historical materialism) is made explicit. In Chapter 13 of *Capital,* Vol. I, Marx states that: "When [. . .] the variation of labor now imposes itself only as an overpowering law of nature with the blindly destructive action of a law of nature, encountering resistance everywhere, through its catastrophes modern industry itself makes it a matter of life and death to recognize variation of labor, and therefore the greatest possible versatility of the laborers, as a universal social law of production; and also to adapt the circumstances of production to the normal operation of this law. Modern industry makes it a matter of life and death to replace the enormity of a suffering working population that is disposable and kept in reserve for the changing needs of capitalist exploitation, by the absolute readiness of man for a variety of work; to replace the part-man, the mere detail-worker in society, by the fully developed individual for whom his various social functions are reciprocally effective modes of his whole activity." [61] Iring Fetscher comments accordingly: "The 'complete man' postu-

60. *Ibid.*
61. MA, Vol. 4, pp. 572 ff.

lated by the early Marx as the counterpart of man impoverished and restricted in development by the division of labor, becomes here an eventual necessary product of the capitalist mode of production itself." [62] However, in contradistinction to Fetscher's supposition, the point of this passage does not seem to me to be that it testifies to Marx's continued attachment to the "humanist intentions" of his early work, but that in it the concept of the "complete man" itself undergoes modification, so that what the young Marx saw as the decisive aspect of the substantive freedom of a *"citoyen"* is now eliminated. The young Marx's criticism of the "complementary abstractness" [63] of the liberal—and Hegel's—conception of a free society is revoked (if this somewhat paradoxical way of expressing it is permissible) not by the late Marx himself but by the perfected reference-system of historical materialism: it can, so to speak, no longer *be formulated*. The remaining "existentially necessary" specifications of the post-capitalist mode of production—the total social regulation of production, the development of "total" individuals, the "cooperative nature of the process of labor" [64]—are not enough to make the reconciliation of what is practically necessary with objectifiable historical necessity seem reasonable.

Particularly worthy of note in the passages from *The German Idealogy* that I have referred to is that they not only reveal the transition from an interpretation of the revolutionary transformation of society that merely caps Hegel's logic of history, to an historico-materialistic understanding of this transformation, but make evident the gap in Marx's theory between the philosophy of history and criticism. At such points Marx's argument would seem through some tacit compulsion to be dually grounded, because only thus can the utopian goal be read in the lines of technical-economic necessity. In reality, the historico-

62. Iring Fetscher, *Karl Marx und der Marxismus* (Munich, 1967), p. 30.
63. Cf. Fetscher, *op. cit.*, pp. 33 ff.
64. Cf. MA, Vol. 4, p. 443.

philosophical schema of interpretation, which is dominated by the logic of production, no longer admits of a formulation of problems of the social system in which questions of survival also appear as questions of the "good life." It suppresses the dimension of historical development essential to such a formulation. Consequently, it no longer allows distinctions which are nevertheless held to be matters of necessity: for example, the distinction between an existentially necessary "socialism" and the socialism of the realm of freedom—and only on that account is it possible for this schema of interpretation to conceive the realm of freedom in the same continuum of historical necessity as the destruction of liberal capitalism. In this kind of system of reference what actually can be said never measures up to all that ought to be said; equivocations and false identifications have to be introduced. Because the existentially necessary new order of production is made equivalent to the commonwealth of freedom, the objective possibility and the practical necessity of enlightening the proletariat about its social situation become the historical (existential) necessity that the proletariat comprehends its own situation, which in the end turns into the necessity that the proletariat will actually achieve the revolutionary goal—the building of the classless society—already "irrevocably ordained" in its present situation. It is evident that (and how) the objectivistic traces in Marx's theory are at one and the same time remnants of an unresolved speculative logic of history with a naturalistic-utopian twist.

5.

In Marx's later writings the problematic aspect of his thought that I have examined up to this point on the whole recedes, to the extent that Marx now distinguishes more precisely between the "spontaneously" advancing, and therefore theoretically objectifiable, process of transformation of capitalist society itself, and the process of the revolutionary abolition of capitalist private property—a process that is merely open to anticipation, because it is practical and political. However, the problem merely recedes; it does not disappear, as can be seen in particular from certain contexts of argument in the *Grundrisse*. There Marx describes the process of dissolution of the liberal capitalist system in terms of scientific and technical progress induced by this system itself; that is, as the "transformation of the process of production from the simple labor process into a scientific process"; the difficulty that arises here is analogous to that analyzed above. On the one hand, Marx describes the process of transformation of capitalism as if capitalism itself, by reason of its own inherent dynamics, must lead to a transcendence of those conditions that constituted the capitalist order of production: alienated labor, exploitation by capital of labor power bought like a commodity, the automatic anarchy of the process of production. On the other hand, however, he allows no doubt about the definite qualitative difference between a production process "made scientific" under the marginal conditions of capitalism, and a socialist order of production resulting from the revolutionary abolition of private capital. The difficulty is evident in the precarious interrelation of both these methods of description.[65]

First of all, let us examine Marx's presentation of the scientific transformation of the process of production as the *dissolution* of the capitalist system of production. This process of reform is reflected in the changed role of directly productive work: "To the degree that modern industry [. . .] develops, the creation of real wealth will depend less on working time and the quantity of applied work, and more on the power of the agencies put into operation during working time, which itself (whose powerful effectiveness) is unrelated to the direct working time which its production requires, but on the contrary depends on the general state of science and on the advance of technology, or the application of this science to production.

65. Cf. Jürgen Habermas, *op. cit.*

[. . .] Labor no longer appears so much as part of the process of production, as man instead acts as the supervisor and regulator of the production process. (What is true for machinery is also valid for the combination of human activities and the development of human intercourse.)" [66] Here Marx is describing a process of "rationalization," which not only basically changes the direct material process of production (and with it the nature of direct labor and of *capital fixe*), inasmuch as he replaces human labor power by an "automatic system of machinery," [67] but then cannot but affect the social intercourse of men, and ultimately must unite men as a species subject to the extent that they have brought external nature under the control of their "general intellect." "In this transformation it is neither the direct labor which man himself carries out, nor the time he works, but the appropriation of his own general productive power, his understanding of nature and the control of nature through his existence as a social unit—in short the development of the social individual, which appears as the major foundation of production and riches. [. . .] As soon as labor has ceased in a direct form to be the major source of riches, working time ceases and must cease to be its yardstick, and therefore exchange value to be that of use value. [. . .] Hence the production dependent on exchange value collapses, and the direct process of material production itself freed from the condition of need and antagonism. The free development of individualities, and therefore not the reduction of necessary working time for surplus work, but above all the reduction of the necessary work of society to a minimum, answered by the aesthetic, scientific or other cultivation of individuals through the time that has become free for them all and through the means provided. [. . .] The development of *capital fixe* shows to what degree universal social knowing, knowledge, has become *direct productive force,* and therefore

66. *Grundrisse* . . . , p. 592.
67. *Ibid.,* p. 587.

108

the conditions for the process of social life itself have come under the control of general intellect, and have been remodelled in accordance with it; to what extent the social productive forces are produced, not only in the form of knowledge, but as direct organs of societal *praxis:* of the actual process of life." [68]

In this version, with the scientific rationalization of production, and the development of the "social individual," the production dependent on exchange value must come to an end. Capital, as the "processual contradiction" as which it intrudes in order to reduce working time to a minimum, whereas on the other hand it posits working time as the only yardstick for and source of wealth, is, on this interpretation, so to speak only the final institutional barrier, which has to fall sooner or later, and whose fall must bring the process of social life completely under the control of the "general intellect," that in all its essential determinations already exists in society. The qualitative transformation, which was always concomitant with the idea of a transcendence of capitalist private ownership, is now incorporated into the one-dimensional advance of a process of rationalization, at the end of which the process of social life will be organized wholly in accordance with the same principles of technical rationality which are at present already largely at work in the organization of the process of production. The model taken as a basis here is not that of a practical reason that becomes actual in non-coercive communication and cooperation, but that of a technical rationality opposed to and controlling nature and society alike: the factor determining the possibility of the effective operation of this rationality is not unobstructed communication, but the occupation of positions of power. Therefore private property appears here as the obstruction which has only to be removed and which inevitably will be removed, in order to provide "general intellect" with the basis of unobstructed efficacy, that is, embracing all processes of social life. Significantly, in the context in question, Marx characterizes the tran-

68. *Ibid.,* pp. 593 ff.

sition from the capitalist to the socialist order of production as the transformation of "surplus work" into "disposable time"; the "contradiction" of the capitalist mode of production consists in the fact that, with the reduction of necessary working time it also increases surplus labor and makes it a condition of necessary labor,[69] whereas under the conditions of socialist production the time given to surplus work would belong to the individual himself, whose freedom and riches would consist precisely therein. "A nation is truly rich when six hours are worked in place of twelve. *Wealth* is not command over surplus working time, but *disposable time* outside that used in direct production, for *each individual* and the whole society." [70] I shall return to the problematics of this conception of the riches of freedom. It seems evident that in this system of reference the transformation of surplus working time into "disposable time" could be wholly the result of a "rendering scientific" of the process of production carried out by administrative means; the emancipation of individuals would then, in fact (in the sense of my initial thesis), be conceivable as the result of a scientifically directed reorganization of society by means of a revolutionary minority governing through an authoritarian regime.

The premisses of his interpretation of history clearly require Marx to consider the intended "process of rationalization" of society in a continuum with the process of rationalization that actually takes place under conditions of capitalist production; and, indeed, in the historical continuum of a progressive increase in labor productivity, in which the resolution of problems of the capitalist system appears just as necessary as the resolution of all system problems hitherto, and in which the qualitative distinction between the two modes of rationalization is at the most permissible as the finding that in socialism the social production process as a whole—with the help of the now established science of society—can be brought under control.

69. Cf. *ibid.*, p. 593.
70. Cf. *ibid.*, p. 594.

On the other hand, even where Marx works on the basis of the qualitative difference between the capitalist and the socialist forms of "rationalization," his argument is remarkably ambivalent or imprecise. At one point in the *Grundrisse,* he appears at first to demonstrate this distinction in developing the determining factors of alienated labor in the case of a production already subjected to scientific rationalization: "In fact, in the capitalist production process, [. . .] labor is a totality—a combination of various forms of labor—the individual components of which are alienated from one another, so that labor as a whole, as a totality, is *not* the *work* of the individual worker, and is only the work of the various workers taken together, insofar as they are combined, in the sense that they do not behave towards one another as if they were united. In their combination, this labor appears both to be performed in the service of an alien will and an alien intelligence, and directed by that alien intelligence—it seems to have a *spiritual unity* external to the labor itself, just as in its material unity it is subjected to the *objective unity* of *machinery,* of *capital fixe,* which as a *terrifying animate colossus* objectifies scientific thought and is in actuality the subsuming whole, but is in no way a mere tool for the individual worker; on the contrary, the individual worker exists, an individual animate punctuality, as an isolated living accessory to this whole. Combined labor is therefore in two aspects combination *in itself;* not combination as the mutual relationship of the individuals engaged in work together, nor as their extension, whether beyond their specific or isolated function or beyond the instrument of labor. Therefore if the worker treats the product of his labor as something alien, it is just as true that he treats combined labor as something alien, even as he treats his own labor as something which indeed pertains to him but is essentially an enforced expression of life and alien to him, and which Adam Smith therefore conceives as a *burden, sacrifice,* and so on." [71]

71. *Grundrisse . . .* , p. 374.

The meaning of this critique of alienated labor under the conditions of machinery (as already developed) seems at first to have a clear meaning: that is, as a negative description offering an implicit characterization of the state of things when alienation is transcended. However, in the later sections in which Marx describes in greater detail the process of scientific rationalization of production, the local value of this criticism changes to a considerable extent. Now the determinations of alienated labor appear *in toto* as those of the automated production process itself: no longer as the attributes of capital, insofar as "it is in its way the appropriation of living labor," but above all as its attributes, insofar as in "its physical aspect" it has become mechanized.[72] The "animate monster" in contrast to which "living work" becomes "a mere live accessory," is the machinery itself as the "technological application of science." [73] "The activity of the worker, restricted to a mere abstraction of activity, is in all its aspects determined and controlled by the movement of machinery, not the other way round. Science [!] which, through proficient automatic design, compels the inanimate part of the mechanism into motion, does not exist in the consciousness of the worker, but operates on him through the machine as an alien force, as the power of the machine itself." [74] Therefore the fact that the workers do not "combine" but are "combined" no longer appears as a characteristic of the capitalist context of relations, but as that of the "automatic system of machinery." Labor "appears only as a conscious organ" distributed "at several points in the mechanical system in individual human workers," subsumed under the total process of the machinery itself, which is itself only a part of the system, the unity of which does not exist in the live workers but in the living (active) machinery which, in "contrast to the [worker's] individual, insignificant action seems to him a powerful orga-

72. Cf. *ibid.,* p. 585.
73. *Ibid.,* p. 587.
74. *Ibid.,* p. 584.

nism." [75] Consequently even the lack of connection between human work, the use value of the things it produces, and the requirements of the producer, is ascribed—independently of the capital relationship—to the machinery itself: "Through the immense mass production possible with machinery, the product is devoid of any reference to the direct needs of the producer, and therefore to direct use value." [76]

This alteration of the line of argument is important, because with it Marx disavows the conception he still held in *The German Ideology,* according to which emancipation would necessarily mean that the realm of freedom would coincide with the realm of necessity: originally this was all that the "transcendence of alienated labor" meant. The new insight is that even in an emancipated society traces of "alienation" must inevitably be found in socially *necessary* work,[77] to the extent that it remains necessary work—necessary for the production of what society requires in order to live. But if, consequently, the abolition of capitalist private ownership can no longer be described as inherently a qualitative change in the sphere of the labor process, the question of exactly *what* it can and must be anticipated *as,* becomes all the more pressing. Here we are referred back to our initial context: for now Marx sees the basic determining factors of the emancipated society as the total social regulation of the process of production and the reduction of working time. But, as we saw, restriction to these conditions alone already decided that the revolutionary transformation of society could be conceived independently of the production of a democratic public attainable only by enlightenment and collective emancipation, and precisely because of this the revolutionary trans-

75. *Ibid.,* p. 585.
76. *Ibid.*
77. And not only because "surplus work" must necessarily be carried out in the emancipated society as well. It is characteristic that, according to Marx, a direct relation between surplus work and alienation of labor can be asserted only insofar as the workers are defrauded of their free time. Cf. MA, Vol. 6, pp. 670 ff.

formation of society could be represented as "historically" necessary. This process of emancipation dependent on enlightenment and political *praxis* is replaced in the *Grundrisse* (perhaps the most interesting point in the whole affair, and one which brings us back to the passage in *The German Ideology* discussed above) by a process of emancipation of the worker occurring exclusively in the sphere of alienated work itself and so to speak complementary to alienation—a process of his emancipation as a "social individual," as which he even now relates to "the production process [only as] its guardian and regulator." This development of the social individual, "his comprehension of nature and its domination through his existence as a social body" appears as the "newly developed" basis of wealth, "brought about by modern industry itself," in contrast to which the old basis appears as "theft of others' working time," as "something wretched." [78] Therefore the form of production dependent on exchange value *must* collapse. In the end, there is an unnoticed blurring of the distinctions between a revolutionary transformation and an organic metamorphosis of the capitalist system: "Thereby the ultimate form of slavery assumed by human activity, that of wage labor on the one hand and that of capital on the other, is destroyed, and this destruction itself is the result of the mode of production corresponding to capital; the material and spiritual conditions of the negation of wage labor and of capital, which are themselves the negation of earlier forms of enforced social production, are themselves results of its process of production." [79] In this apocryphal connection, Marx no longer develops the dialectics of alienation and emancipation from the context of capital itself (namely, as a movement culminating in a "practical" process of emancipation), but from the transformation (only mediated by capital) of the material process of production as such. Therefore the central determination of "alienation" (in the original sense) remains theft

78. Cf. *op. cit.,* p. 593.
79. Cf. *Grundrisse* . . . , p. 635.

of other men's working time; and the total social regulation of production becomes the fundamental condition of emancipation: above all, because it alone can bring about the *possible* radical "reduction of the working day" as the basis of the realm of freedom *beyond* the sphere of material production.[80] Therefore the realm of freedom remains bound up with the realm of necessity, but in a very precarious fashion, as will now become clear from consideration of a well-known, pertinent passage in *Capital.*

This sudden transition from the *Grundrisse* to *Capital* should not allow the profound differences between the official and an apocryphal version of the theory of collapse to be hidden. At the points in *Capital,* where—so to speak—*economic* reasons replace technological reasons, the above critique is of course not applicable; but this does not make it invalid, for the theoretical connection to which it refers is also latent in *Capital,* namely, as the attempt to conceive the transition from capitalist to socialist society as historically necessary on the basis of laws of economic movement; but, in particular, Marx's statements about the realm of freedom accord straightforwardly with the theoretical relation in question. In these statements Marx might be said to present the implications of his analysis in the *Grundrisse* of the scientific rationalization of the production process: "The realm of freedom actually begins only where the labor determined by need and external expediency ends. Therefore it is by its very nature outside the sphere of material production proper. Just as the savage has to wrestle with nature in order to satisfy his needs, to maintain and to reproduce his life, so is the case with civilized man, who must do so in all forms of society and under all possible modes of production." [81] Only beyond the sphere of material production, which in all forms

80. Cf. MA, Vol. 6, p. 672.
81. MA, Vol. 6, p. 671.

of society must remain a "realm of necessity," "begins the development of human powers as an end in itself, the true realm of freedom, which, however, can bloom only upon that realm of necessity as its basis." [82] Marx now distinguishes very precisely between the *basis* of the realm of freedom to be established in the abolition of private capital brought about by revolution, and the realm of freedom itself (not to be brought about, but to be "delivered" through revolution) only in which the full wealth of human relations and human self-realizations can unfold and flourish. But how is the relation between them to be comprehended? The realm of freedom cannot be a reality, that is, it cannot be the expression of the freedom of associated individuals in regard to their own history, if it is not a reality in the *basis* as well, that is, if it is not mediated with the realm of necessity in the organization of the social reproduction process. In fact, the decisive qualitative difference between the capitalist and socialist social systems must reside primarily in the differing forms of organization of the "realm of necessity." Where then is the freedom in the realm of necessity, and in what does it consist? "Freedom in this area," says Marx, "can consist only in the fact that socialized man, the associated producers, control their interplay with nature rationally, bringing it under their common control, instead of being dominated by it as if by a blind power, and operating it with the smallest possible expenditure of energy and under conditions that are most worthy of and appropriate to their nature as human beings." [83]

Here Marx describes the freedom of associated producers in regard to their interchange with nature, with which at the same time a new mode of history is born, as the overthrow of a master-slave relationship. Instead of being ruled by the production process as by a blind power, men will bring it under their common control. But that is to interpret the dissolution of *social* master-slave relationships on the lines of the "mastery,"

82. *Ibid.*
83. *Ibid.,* p. 671.

116

or conquest, of nature. The implications have to be made clear.

If Marx had described the establishment and dissolution of social relations of domination as phases of a struggle for recognition, to be followed by the reciprocal recognition of the many in their own right as proven individuals, it would be evident that what he describes here as the "common control" of the production process belonged wholly to neither the realm of necessity nor that of freedom. For "communality" cannot reside only in the way in which the necessary is regulated, rather it must be at the same time the way in which what is necessary is decided. In other words: the explication of what "common control" would have to mean would be the explanation of what would happen within the political scope of a liberated populace, if the "united individuals" were to settle, in free discussion, the dialectics between what they are capable of technically, and what they want in practice. Marx, on the other hand, reduces the social practice of "associated producers" to control of the production process, to the same extent that he grounds their association in the oneness of the "general intellect" by which they master nature. Therefore that component in which the association itself must always recur is, as it were, subjected to the *praxis* of the associated individuals; the association appears as a preordained fact, and not as a form of the social life process itself. Hence freedom in the realm of necessity can only be the knowledge of necessity; but that means the installation of "general intellect" as an automatic control system.

The inadequacy of Marx's interpretation of history is once again reflected in his distinction between the realm of freedom and the realm of necessity, and in his mediation of the two. The realm of freedom, which this interpretation declares would have to result from the resolution of the problems of the capitalist system, could also be a realm of areas of private latitude in a social reproduction process steered by a rationality on a basis of purely technical organization, and obeying "regularities peculiar to" technico-scientific progress. But then it would be an

117

adequate condition for emancipation if the revolutionary proletariat (or its advance guard) captured the control centers from
which the degree of technico-organizational rationality necessary for industrial society could be exerted in the over-all planning of the production process; since the question of *what* was
necessary would appear "scientifically" determinable, it would
be decided by the new technocrats who would only be manag-
ing things. The freedom of individuals living in this kind of
emancipated society would not be the freedom of autonomous
individuals in a humanized history, but the free *time* of "domes-
ticated farm animals" and "laboratory rats" in the "controlled
life-system of a controlled environment." [84] In order to accept
this caricature of the realm of freedom, one would have in fact
to demythologize the utopian idea of a realization of philosophy
all over again—to the point of making it a negative utopia. And
practical reason would finally be left wandering in a no man's
land between necessity and illusory freedom.

Even though these implications may contradict Marx's intentions, they are *possible* consequences of the relationship between the role of the concept of labor in Marx's theory, his
interpretation of history, his understanding of science, and the
indications of an objectivistic bias in his theory of revolution.
In this context, the decisive distinctions between the *minimal*
and the optimal conditions of survival in industrial society are
effaced in Marx's theory; the realm of freedom becomes what
this society has to achieve in order to ensure the bare means
of survival itself. However, some of Marx's disciples have taken
this to mean that the "association of individuals" will be the
(in the long run) inevitable result of the process of revolutionary change, thus allowing questions of revolutionary strategy to
become in fact questions of a "technically" defined expediency
and proficiency on the way to the assumption of power by the
organized guard of the proletariat. In this conception, the an-

84. Cf. Herbert Marcuse, *Versuch über die Befreiung* (Frankfurt,
1969).

swers history itself has given to the question of the "good life" must of necessity be acknowledged as the right answers. Existing socialism then becomes true socialism, and every objection individuals whose rights are encroached upon or violated make against the technocrats administering historical necessity becomes the expression of a false consciousness. On the other hand, in the same context the relation of Marx's theory to capitalism stabilizing itself through political reorganization becomes equivocal: either this readjustment contradicts the theory, or it must, from the viewpoints of stability and economic growth, be permitted as a legitimate rival to socialism. For the one-dimensional nature of Marx's idea of history implies a one-dimensional idea of technical progress, the sheer factual existence, and no longer the quality, of which becomes the decisive criterion of progressiveness.

119

3. CRITIQUE OF INSTRUMENTAL REASON AND CRITICAL SOCIAL THEORY

Marx assumed not only that the peculiar nature of the capitalist production process would cause it to reach a point of crisis, but that the arrival of this crisis would be one with the development of the material and spiritual (which means also the necessary and sufficient) prerequisites for a socialist revolution. His assumption proved false, and in a fatal sense. The great social revolutions of this century occurred in countries with predominantly agricultural economies, whereas, despite catastrophic crises, the major capitalist states were able to recover their political stability. The result is a world-political stage with structures and tendencies, actors, spheres of action and emancipatory potentials that have become increasingly difficult to analyze in terms of a critique of political economy.

Since history itself has thoroughly discredited all hopes of an economically grounded "mechanism" of emancipation, it is not only necessary for a theoretical analysis to take into account entirely new constellations of "bases" and "superstructures": in fact, the criticism and alteration of the "superstructure" have a new and decisive importance for the movements of liberation. In order to reformulate Marx's supposition about the prerequisites for a successful revolution in the case of the capitalist countries, it would be necessary to include socialist democracy, socialist justice, socialist ethics and a "socialist consciousness" among the components of a socialist society to be "incubated"

121

within the womb of a capitalist order. In short, elements that would have to be included are institutions, forms of life, political *praxis,* that could become the nucleus of a new, emancipated organization of social life, and the nucleus of a new "public freedom." Therefore the criteria of "revolutionary practice" in non-revolutionary times would have essentially to be determined by the practical necessity of advancing the abolition of repression under repressive conditions, that is, of developing the elements of a new, democratically constituted society in "the womb of the old society" by the transformation of consciousness, practice and institutions. But, under the conditions of organized capitalism, this would mean that processes of enlightenment, a *praxis* of radical reform only indirectly negating the boundary conditions of the system, and political struggle in the sense of all activable tendencies immanent to the system which are capable of advancing the spontaneity, sensibility, autonomy and political consciousness of individuals, the removal of illusive legitimations for the continuation of manipulative conditions and undemocratic procedures of decision, and the extension of public spheres of emanicipation, obtain decisive significance. In this way, Marx's criticism of political moralism would be turned upside down again, *to the extent that* the Enlightenment, *in opposition* to the historically effective tendencies towards the complete dehumanization of human social life, had to bring to conscious recognition the objective possibility and the practical necessity of an ultimate resolution by men, through rational *praxis,* of the historically and laboriously won promise of public freedom and individual happiness in a society of emancipated citizens.

As we have seen, an historico-anthropological prejudice is at the basis of the affirmative trend of Marx's philosophy of history, according to which the revolution should become the conscious execution of the tendencies of modern history which prevail spontaneously in the capitalist industrialization process. This prejudice conceals the specific gravity and particular difficulties of the revolutionary task, which is to realize the "realm of freedom," in practice, as a sphere of public freedom—that is, as a community of mature citizens; and conceals it to the same extent as the dangers of a bureaucratic and technocratic centralism and dehumanizing consequences of an autonomous "rationalization process." As far as *this* point is concerned, the anarchists would seem to have shown more understanding of historical realities.[1] And the communes and soviets which arose for the most part spontaneously in the course of two French

1. Cf. the *Zirkular der Sechzehn* (Circular Letter of the Sixteen), against which Marx and Engels (primarily, of course, on acceptable political grounds) argue in *Die angeblichen Spaltungen der Internationale* (The Alleged Dissensions of the International): "How is it possible to ensure that a society of equality and freedom arises from an authoritarian organization? It is impossible. The International, the seed of the human society of the future, must henceforth become the faithful image of our principles of freedom and federation" (MEW, Vol. 18, p. 43). On the other hand, Marx and Engels stress the need for a disciplined—under certain conditions even an armed—political struggle; by reason of which necessity the International could not possibly be the "image of the New Jerusalem." Admittedly, this is only half the truth, for Marx and Engels fail to appreciate the aspect of truth in the anarchists' attack on the International precisely because their "model of the revolution" is that of a transformation of "functions of government" into "simple administrative functions." Hence, for them, the question of the right organizational structure of the International is reduced, potentially at least, to a search for the appropriate means "of destroying the coercive measures of social and political power concentrated in the hands of the exploiters" (MEW, Vol. 18, p. 50). I repeat—potentially. On other occasions Marx had opposed the anarchists wholly on the basis of their own arguments, as, for instance, when he criticized Bakunin's organizational proposals as "Jesuitical," and put forward "publicity" and "discussion" as the principles of organization of the International which could alone ensure "unity of thought and action" (MEW, Vol. 18, p. 346). Occasionally, in the course of their polemics against the anarchists, Marx and Engels reply in directly "moral" terms ("The International requires of all its adherents an acknowledgement of *truth, justice and morality* as the guiding principles of their behavior: but the alliance [. . .]" *ibid.*, p. 372); but, so it seems to me, they never discussed the question of the connection between the organizational forms of the revolutionary movement and the goal of the revolution on the level of principle, on which the anarchists at first considered it. For Marx and Engels the anarchistic trauma of a post-revolutionary *authoritarian* administrative state remained only, so it would appear, an infantile delusion. See also Engels' polemic against the "anti-authoritarians," the undeniable realism of which now appears highly ambivalent (F. Engels, *Von der Autorität*, MEW, Vol. 18, pp. 305–308).

123

and two Russian revolutions were first attempts at practical solutions of an historical task, the nature of which was remarkably misconstrued by the leading theoreticians of revolutionary socialism: I refer here to the task of removing, along with precapitalist and capitalist forms of the exploitation of men by men, *all* forms of exploitation and domination.[2]

2. Marx himself, of course, exalted the Paris Commune as "the political form at last discovered under which the economic emancipation of labor could be realized" (*Adresse des Generalrates über den Bürgerkrieg in Frankreich 1871* [*The Civil War in France*], MA, Vol. 3, 2, p. 927); the Commune had, Marx emphasizes, "supplied the Republic with the basis of really democratic institutions" (*ibid.*, p. 926). Behind this was certainly the knowledge that economic emancipation could be realized on the basis of political democracy only *as* human emancipation, and that *consequently* "the working class cannot simply lay hold of the ready-made state machinery, and operate it for its own purposes" (*ibid.*, p. 919). But this insight appears at this point in Marx's writings only in a peculiarly attenuated form. He speaks of the Communual Constitution mainly as a *means* of removing class rule, but not as an *anticipation* of the future Republican Constitution, under which form it would have represented the necessary union of economic and political emancipation: "The Commune would therefore serve as a lever to overthrow the economic foundations on which the existence of classes, and therefore class rule, rests" (*ibid.*, p. 927). Here again, unawares, there comes to the forefront the idea that economic emancipation is to be comprehended as something independent of the democratization of society; the relationship between the "economic emancipation of labor" and the establishment of a truly democratic Republic is therefore represented not as a reciprocal but ultimately as a unilaterally determined relationship; hence Marx can say of the Commune: "Neither 'cheap government' nor the 'true Republic' was its ultimate aim; they were its mere concomitants" (*ibid.*, p. 926). In view of the failure of the Paris Commune, Marx was able later to present the primary requirements as "the most decisive centralization of force in the hands of the state power" as against the "democratic talk of the freedom of communes, self-government, and so on." Although the abrogation of political domination remained for Marx the obvious goal of the revolution, Oskar Anweiler is not wholly unjustified in suggesting that "for Marx, the revolutionary communes are no more than temporary instruments of struggle to advance the Revolution," and that Marx "did not see them as the germ-cells of a fundamental transformation of society, which would instead come from above, through the centralized proletarian state power" (O. Anweiler, *Die Rätebewegung in Russland* 1905–1921; ref. in Arendt, *op. cit.*, p. 330; see also, pp. 329 f.).

124

In her perception of the specific nature of this historical task, Rosa Luxemburg seems entitled to a special place among the revolutionary theoreticians of the periods before World War I and during the Revolution. Even in 1904 she criticized Lenin's "ultra-centralism" as a "Blanquist" deviation, that is, as the expression of a conspiratorial strategy for the seizure of power, which was incompatible with the political aims of a proletarian revolution.[3] Here she could still base her case essentially on Marx, for Lenin's strategy was conceivable only in a country with a poorly developed capitalist mode of production and a correspondingly weakly developed industrial proletariat: it was an attempt to use strict forms of political organization to compensate for the absence of revolutionary conditions that were, according to Marx, indispensable. The originality of Rosa Luxemburg's political ideas therefore only became clearly apparent at the moment when, after the Revolution, she repeated her objection as a criticism of the dictatorial centralism of the revolutionary regime. Here and there this criticism becomes an ardent plea for "public freedoms" and democratic institutions: "The only way to rebirth is the school of public life itself, the most unrestricted form of democracy, public opinion, [. . .] Without universal suffrage, unrestricted liberty of the press and assembly, and a free exchange of opinion, life withers in every public institution and becomes an illusion of life in which bureaucracy remains the sole active element."[4]

Behind Rosa Luxemburg's words, one can sense the shock with which Western European socialists must have discovered that what they (like Marx, far too deeply grounded in the political traditions of Western Europe) had always held to be self-evident, was nothing of the sort; and that the proletarian revolution was not the *realization* of the democratic tendencies

3. Cf. Rosa Luxemburg, "Organisationsfragen der russischen Sozialdemokratie," in *Politische Schriften*, Vol. 3 (Frankfurt and Vienna, 1968), pp. 83 ff.
4. Rosa Luxemburg, *Die russische Revolution*, p. 136.

of the modern European constitutional state, but their *abrogation*. It is instructive to read Rosa Luxemburg's criticism against the background of our critique of Marx up to this point. Basically, she accuses Lenin's theory of dictatorship of conceiving the organization of the "basis" of the realm of freedom as a technical-administrative problem, and not as the practical task of the "realization of socialism" itself as an "economic, social and just system"; "something that lies wholly in the mists of the future." [5] Rosa Luxemburg understands the expropriation by force of the capitalist class as it must actually be comprehended in accordance with the ideology-critical approach of Marx's theory: as the purely *negative* condition for the realization of socialism, which (and here she restores to validity an insight repressed even by Marx) can be conceived only as the practical project of individuals emancipating themselves in democratized institutions and united by the bond of a liberated public life. She is also criticizing Marx, even if in a very indirect manner, and unintentionally, when she writes: "It is the historic task of the proletariat, when it takes power, to establish socialist democracy in place of bourgeois democracy—not any form of democracy. But socialist democracy does not begin in the promised land, when the infrastructure of a socialist economy has been established, as a finished gift for the good people who in the meantime have faithfully supported a handful of socialist dictators. Socialist democracy starts with the removal of class domination *and* the construction of socialism. It starts in the moment in which the socialist party takes power. It is the dictatorship of the proletariat." [6]

The Bolsheviks came to power with the slogan "All power to the soviets!" But this affirmation arose neither from a theoretical insight, nor as the expression of a Party tradition. Instead it corresponded to the incorporation of the soviet movement, which spread spontaneously during the Revolution, into a stra-

5. *Ibid.,* p. 134.
6. *Ibid.,* p. 139.

tegic concept, in which the Party's monopoly of power was in the end more important than the democratization of public life. Without making light of the enormous difficulties that the Russian revolutionaries had to face when their revolution had failed to ignite a revolution throughout Europe, it is permissible to impute to its advance a certain inner logic, which shows in the fact that, under the first onslaught of problems that hit the construction of socialism in an underdeveloped, isolated and threatened country, these revolutionaries abandoned the democratic principles of the Soviet constitution as quickly as they had previously accepted them. In this perspective, Stalinism becomes no more than an inhuman and so to say pathological form of Leninism. It is futile to argue about the extent to which, despite all this, the October Revolution was the great breakthrough of socialism; futile, because the balance sheet can no longer be made up: that is, the fate of European socialism without the spectre of a Red terror, on one hand, and without the rigidification of the Communist movements of Western Europe directed from the Soviet H.Q., on the other.

I have attempted, in conjunction with the previous criticism of Marx, to indicate once more the historical background against which Western European intellectuals have tried since the twenties to bring an "unmodified" Marx into currency again, in contrast to ossified official Party discussion. Since then, "critical Marxism" has become a privileged possession of radical intellectuals, at first in the capitalist countries and, since the end of World War II, to an increasing extent in the socialist countries too. The isolation of this critical Marxism from political *praxis* has begun to give way only in the last few years. One characteristic seems to be common despite all fundamental differences, from Korsch, the philosophers of the Frankfurt School, Sartre and Marcuse, to the theoreticians of the Marxism of Warsaw, Prague and Zagreb: that, as the expression of oppositionist

127

tendencies, it is required implicitly or explicitly to oppose the objectivistic trends of Marx's philosophy of history; that it espouses the claims of individuals to autonomy and happiness as against the historically effective tendencies to the totalization of technical and bureaucratic rationality; that (here quite un-Marxist) it espouses "morality" as against the "course of the world." This post-revolutionary critical Marxism has as yet led to no theory that (in regard to historical concretion and empirical contents) can be put side by side with that of Marx. Nevertheless, taken as a whole, it is yet another confirmation of the need for an ideology-critical examination of Marx's theory itself, which (with the acumen of the conservative) Hans Freyer expressed forty years ago. In Marx's intensification of "Hegel's ethics as naturalism," and in his turning of the " 'necessity of the cause,' that is, the necessity of reason, into the causal mechanism of social movement," [7] Freyer hears the call-sign of an age which "applied all forms of thought, particularly those inherited from German idealism (having wrested them into a naturalistic shape), to all areas of reality, even to social facts and the forms of thought proper to the physical sciences." [8] However overstated this criticism may be, the "possibility of establishing a just society" [9] is in fact a prejudgement that puts Marxist theory (to a greater extent than its creators would have wished) in line with the other great sociological "draft theories" of the nineteenth century—but now in a negative sense: "As every social reality is, so it thinks." [10]

I shall now return to the Frankfurt school's critique of positivism and make use of these last insights. At the beginning of this essay, I presented the early Horkheimer's theory, corresponding to the contemporary self-conception of Marxist intellectuals, from the viewpoint of a return to the "authentic,"

7. Hans Freyer, *Soziologie als Wirklichkeitswissenschaft,* p. 296.
8. *Ibid.,* p. 284.
9. Cf. *ibid.,* p. 70.
10. *Ibid.,* p. 284.

"dialectical" Marx. It is now evident that this return was already a wholly critical one. Horkheimer's criticism of capitalist society is already fundamentally a "critique of instrumental reason"; the instrumentalization of reason, which Horkheimer observed in bourgeois science, is perceived to be the interdiction of reason in view of the increasingly universal growth of conditions of domination, and the exchange principle of bourgeois society is interpreted as the fullest expression of this instrumentalized reason. Already implicit here is a criticism of the objectivistic tendencies of Marx's conception of revolution; it appears in the distinction between different forms of revolutionary struggle, in the criticism of the bureaucratic rigidity of the socialist movement, in the demand for the union of spontaneity and discipline and for the anticipation of future solidarity in the organization of the revolutionary struggle, and, finally, in the criticism of the objectivistic "misunderstanding" of Marx's theory itself. What Horkheimer still represents here as a genuine interpretation of Marx, has already been conditioned by the insight that the revolution has to *break through* a closed world of technical rationality and reified relations, and therefore that it does not only have to *carry out* the laws of such a world by means of a mere shifting of the centers of power. Even in the early Horkheimer, the link is broken that in Marx joined the critique of political economy to the theory of revolution. However, this is already a first step towards what proved so characteristic of the later Frankfurt school—the displacement of the critique of political economy by which the main component of a revolutionary theory becomes the instrument of an ideology criticism suspicious of political practice.

In *The Dialectics of Enlightenment*, which Horkheimer and Adorno completed in 1944, while in exile, its authors established the consequences of their critical interpretation of Marx and of recent historical experiences. *The Dialectics of Enlightenment* is a fascinating attempt to produce a profound historico-philosophical critique of capitalist society—so profound

129

that it grapples both with the liberal capitalism criticized by Marx and with its state-capitalist and state-interventionist heirs, and incorporates them in a proficient conceptual framework. Marx saw the cause of the reification of all social relations in the unleasing of the exchange rationality in bourgeois society. Inasmuch as he associated this rationality with a specific form of ownership, he saw the abrogation of this form of property as productive of a consequent removal of reification; therefore, Horkheimer and Adorno detach the criticism of exchange rationality from its fundamental exposition in terms of labor value in the criticism of political economy, and translate it into a criticism of instrumental reason: the criticism of instrumental reason replaces the criticism of political economy in terms of trends, and the criticism of political economy becomes a criticism of technical civilization.

The theoretical significance of this process is immense. The dialectics of alienation and emancipation that Marx identified is now revealed in all its implications, in such a way that the theoretical resolution of this dialectics is shown to be obstructed by a theory of revolution on the Marxian pattern. According to Marx, the social systems produced by men must turn into an external authority over the reified subjects, in order to permit development of the material resources which will ultimately allow men to make their own history with the will and consciousness of freely socialized individuals. However, since for Marx the dialectical union of social existence and consciousness ultimately became a unilateral determining relationship, he could describe the history of self-sacrifice and emancipation only in accordance with that *external* destiny which men were themselves preparing by building a class society; by the same logic of self-preservation that brought men to involve themselves in this external destiny, they must also eventually liberate themselves from it. Horkheimer faced Marx with the other side of the picture. The external fate in which men have had to involve themselves for the sake of emancipation from their natural

130

corruption, is at the same time their inner destiny; a destiny which reason sustains through its own efforts. Ultimately, the subjects for whose sake the subjection, reification and demythization of nature were begun, are themselves so repressed, reified and disenchanted in self regard, that even their emancipatory efforts become the contrary: the confirmation of the context of delusion in which they are imprisoned. The cancellation of an animistic image of the world already saw the foundation of the dialectics of enlightenment which, in capitalist industrial society, is taken to the point where "man is anthropomorphized for man." [11] "The ratio which supplants mimesis is not simply its opposite. It is itself mimesis: mimesis unto death. The subjective spirit which cancels the animation of nature, exerts power over a despiritualized nature only by imitating its rigidity, and despiritualizing itself in turn." [12]

Horkheimer and Adorno (who know their Freud) emphasize that "the power of control over non-human nature and over other men" was repeatedly paid for by the "denial of nature in man." "This very denial, the nucleus of all civilizing rationality, is the cancer-cell of a proliferating mythic irrationality; with the denial of nature in man, not only the goal of the external conquest of nature, but the goal of man's own individual life is distorted and rendered unintelligible. As soon as man discards his awareness that he himself is nature, all the aims for which he goes on living—social progress, the enhancement of all material and spiritual powers, even consciousness itself— are as nothing, and the enthroning of the means as an end (which in late capitalism develops to a degree tantamount to open insanity) is already perceptible even in the prehistory of subjectivity. Man's mastery over himself, which is the basis of his self, is almost without exception the destruction of the individual as subject, thus negating the very purpose of that

11. M. Horkheimer and T. W. Adorno, *Dialektik der Aufklärung* (Amsterdam, 1944), p. 73.
12. *Ibid.*

mastery." [13] Admittedly, just as the productive forces arising under the enslaving pressures of a class society are the condition for social wealth and hence the pre-condition of a state of life without domination, so the subjection of nature in man is the pre-condition of personal autonomy: it is part of the mechanism of formation of an ego-consciousness. But the consequence of the world-historical identity of both processes has been that the reification of individuals has advanced to the same extent as the objectification of external nature; in the end, the individual subjects are no longer there who alone would be able to "appropriate to themselves" the promised social wealth.

Therefore, for Horkheimer and Adorno, "Enlightenment" becomes a world-historical project of the human species, in which the species simultaneous creates itself and threatens its own destruction; its ultimate aim is social freedom, happiness and the independence of the individual, but its secret logic aims at the extinction of the self-liberating subjects and the self-elevation of social bondage and constraint. From this viewpoint, the various metamorphoses of capitalist society that with Marx's approach were equally incomprehensible, can now be shown to be in fact accomplishments of the law of movement of this capitalist society—the ways in which the law of increasing objectification is fulfilled. Odysseus and the Marquis de Sade's Juliette become key figures in a process of enlightenment at the self-destructive end of which enlightenment degenerates into mass deception.

Critical theory therefore establishes, in contradistinction to Marx, that the fateful process of "rationalization" of all processes of social life does not find its preordained end in an emancipated society, but—in accordance with its inward logic—is compelled instead to end in the opposite of emancipation: in the subjection of men, too, to the domination over nature that they themselves have achieved. But then "revolution" is no longer

13. *Op. cit.*, pp. 70 f.

conceivable as the conscious and collective fulfillment of an objectifiable historical necessity. "Revolution" in the sense of a liberation from the natural history of man is far more something which results from an enlightenment of enlightened reason about its own nature—and that something is the *breaking-through* of the dialectics of enlightenment of which revolutions to date were mere blind agents.

This radicalization of Marx's philosophy of history, by means of which (a long way from Marx's "technical humanism" [cf. Klages]) the unleashing of technical rationality is perceived to be the most decisive of all forms of domination of men by men, anticipates some of the basic ideas of Marcuse. It reveals somber prospects for reified men. For their integration into the universal context of delusion is so inclusive that even the most serious efforts of liberation run the danger of confirming and stabilizing the existing power structure. The possibility of a "*praxis* that will bring about a revolutionary transformation" therefore depends on the self-abandonment of the enlightenment in its "positivistic aspect" being comprehended appropriately, and on thought reaching enlightenment about itself when it addresses itself to the domination in itself that is at the same time "nature unreconciled." Only this kind of self-conscious thought, which was from the start the only form in which enlightenment was opposed to domination, Horkheimer and Adorno believe has the power to break through that "necessity" which socialism prematurely glorified as the "guarantor of freedom to come." [14] Critical theory therefore remains the pioneer and conscience of a revolutionary, transforming *praxis*. But the future subjects of that *praxis* are no longer to be discerned so simply; the possibility of their existing is dependent solely on the "intransigence of theory in regard to the lack of consciousness which allows society to adopt an inflexible pattern of thought." [15] With a resignation born of the experience

14. Cf. *op. cit.*, pp. 54 ff.
15. *Ibid.*, p. 56.

of insanity systematized, the authors of *The Dialectics of Enlightenment* come finally to the question of the very possibility of enlightenment: "If it is possible today to speak to anyone [in this regard], then we pass on the responsibility not to the so-called masses, and not to the individual (who is powerless) but to an imaginary witness—lest it disappear with us entirely." [16]

The *Dialectics of Enlightenment* has a key position in regard to the later development of the critical theory of the Frankfurt school. Attention to the basic ideas of these "philosophical fragments" (the sub-title of the book) should help in further elucidation of the problem upon which my meta-theoretical discusion up to now has centered: the question of the mutual relationship of "science" and "criticism." Adorno and Horkheimer take seriously the claim of Marx's theory to the status of ideology criticism; as against Marx's scientistic self-misconception they rely on his declared intention to reveal behind the mere "apparent forms" of capitalist commodity-society its "essential nature"—which means too, its "unnatural essence." [17] This insistence on the distinction between essence and appearance is equally an insistence on the "dual nature" of society *and* sociology, which positivism denies. Adorno remarked on this again in one of his last essays: "Sociology enjoys a dual nature: in it the subject of all knowledge, society, [. .] is simultaneously the object. Society is subjective because it refers back to the men who form it, and also because it refers its principles of organization back to subjective consciousness. [. . .] It is objective, because by reason of its supporting structure its own subjectivity remains unintelligible to it, because it has no total subject and through its organization prevents one from being established. However, a dual nature

16. *Ibid.*, p. 307.
17. Cf. Adorno's Introduction to the collection of essays by various authors, *Der Positivismusstreit in der deutschen Soziologie* (Neuwied and Berlin, 1969), pp. 18 f.

of this kind modifies the attitude of socio-scientific knowledge to its object—a fact that positivism does not acknowledge. It treats society, potentially the self-determining subject, unceremoniously as if it were an object to be determined from without." [18] In this way, the practical core of the theory of science controversy between "traditional" and "critical" theory, to which the early Horkheimer had already referred, is revealed anew: Critical social theory lives by the anticipation of a "total social subject"; only on the basis of this anticipation is it able to conceive the apparent forms of a social disorder or "unnatural essence" of society; the validity of its findings is bound up with the efficacy of a liberating *interest* in cognition—in knowing. Whether sociology "as science is to accept society in the particular form in which it functions in any given case, as it has been traditionally represented as doing from Comte to Talcott Parsons, or whether—from the basis of social experience—it strives for the transformation of its fundamental structures, determines scientific theory in all categories and is therefore scarcely to be decided in terms of scientific theory." [19]

The interplay of "criticism" and "science" can then be more precisely determined than is the case with the relationship between "critical" and "positive" science: that is, criticism is possible only as the *science* of society, since "an unmodified theory of society cannot dispense with laws—those of its structural movement." [20] But this brings us back to the problematics from which Habermas's reflections started out. The critical theory of *The Dialectics of Enlightenment* would occasionally appear to imply that Marx's critique of political economy, after the rejection of its positivistic misinterpretations, could not, as a social theory of society, be empirically refutable in any explicable sense; the historico-philosophical "generalization"

18. *Ibid.*, p. 43.
19. *Ibid.*, p. 79.
20. *Ibid.*, p. 22.

of the criticism of political economy seems in fact to demand an interpretation that would make its basic assumptions none other than those of a criticism of instrumental reason: consequently, they would become a universally applicable key for an ideology-critical "hermeneutics" of the world of social life, precisely through being withdrawn once and for all from scientific criticism. However, such an interpretation would contradict the intention of critical theory to reveal the "laws of movement" of capitalist society; yet this intention is none other than the real meaning of Marx's intention to "make criticism scientific." If this intention is taken seriously, it becomes clear that the philosophical intensification of the criticism of capitalism in *The Dialectics of Enlightenment* is not the *scientific* extension of Marx's theory as an empirical social theory in a practical sense. Hence the need for a more up-to-date "making scientific" of criticism.

Critical theory has to admit (to itself) that the relentless detection of a perverted rationality in all the manifestations of social life does not mean that the society in question has been conceptualized proficiently; therefore critical theory must again in all seriousness re-incorporate those intentions of Marx's and Freud's theories, by which they empirically analyzed the mechanisms of social reproduction so that actual individuals and social groups were able to obtain a partial clarity about their actual historico-social situation that proved fruitful in practice. Like Marx's theory, critical theory must try to analyze the developmental tendencies and mechanisms of the occurrence of politically significant conflicts and systematic problems; and, finally, it must elucidate the objective possibilities of the abolition of domination and false "material pressures." However, a critical societal theory, which would in this sense unite a criticism of instrumental reason with enlightenment regarding the transformed reproductive mechanisms of domination under the conditions of organized capitalism, is available at present

136

only in the form of hypotheses and approaches. The dilemmas of enlightenment which Adorno and Horkheimer mention in *The Dialectics of Enlightenment* are therefore rooted not *only* in the "lack of awareness which allows society's thinking to stultify," but in a deficiency of illuminating "discourse," and in inadequate knowledge in theory.

The "philosophization of *Capital* in the discussions of Marxist intellectuals was a necessary reaction to the bureaucratic ossification and inflexibility of socialism and the rise of a Communist orthodoxy. At the same time, however, it shows that this fascinating instrument of criticsm has become blunt; that Marx's theory of class and of labor value is just as inadequate for a critical and scientific analysis of modern capitalist industrial society as is Lenin's theory of imperialism for an analysis of the relations between the industrial nations and the Third World.[21] This indicates a crisis in socialist theory which, insofar as it is a crisis of identity in the socialist movement itself, is probably more profound than all comparable crises up to the outbreak of World War II. It did not begin in the last few years, but was perceived with full consciousness only with the rise of a New Left insistent that philosophy turn practical. This New Left is the living proof that the criticism of political economy no longer offers any answer in the quest for potentially politicizable, that is, the liberating potentials in society; which means equally: the search for the specific mechanisms of reproduction and transformation, and for the system-problems of modern capitalist society.

I believe that a new theoretical approach such as that of Habermas, in which the intention of criticizing science is joined with that of making criticism scientific, presupposes two things

21. Cf. Jürgen Habermas, *Technik und Wissenschaft als Ideologie* (Frankfurt, 1968); C. Offe, "Herrschaft und Klassenstruktur. Zur Analyse spätkapitalistischer Gesellschaften in *Einführung in die Politikwissenschaft,* ed. D. Senghaas (Frankfurt, 1969).

137

CRITICAL THEORY OF SOCIETY

about this society: (1) that Marx's concept of class has largely lost its utility as an instrument of analysis; and (2) that science has not only become the decisive productive force, but that, together with educational institutions, it represents a decisive critical potential of highly industrialized societies, or can produce this critical potential in the form of scientifically qualified experts from the most varied social strata. If these assumptions are correct, then it is quite obvious that the differences in debate between "critical" and "traditional" science can no longer be interpreted in purely political terms as the expression of a class conflict, but that—precisely for that reason—they can and must be settled on the ground of science itself, because science itself has become the "form of life" of industrial societies, and enlightenment is therefore possible only as an enlightenment of those directly or indirectly participating in science: as enlightenment about the irrationality of a *praxis* whose living element and principle of legitimation is scientific rationality, and as enlightenment about the repression of communication processes whose release alone will provide scientific-technical progress with a rational direction that can satisfy the needs of the individuals who make it advance. This means, however, that in contrast to the early Horkheimer we must assume that the interest in—the will to—liberation will take future effect precisely *in* the scientific and educational system of highly industrialized societies (that is, societies living by science), inasmuch as it is an interest mediated only by this system.

Marx took for granted that he had to submit to the judgment of scientific criticism.[22] His theory was *addressed,* however, to impoverished proletarians, whom we cannot reproach for being content with something less than the commonwealth of freedom. Only in a changed historical situation are the potential critics

22. Cf. the Preface to the first edition of *Capital* (MA, Vol. 4, p. xxi).

of critical social theory those to whom it is addressed, and those to whom it is addressed—increasingly—its potential critics. In this, perhaps we can discern the chance of that actual union of critical theory and liberating practice that both theory and practice hitherto have so often failed to achieve.